Current
CONTROVERSIES

Whistleblowers

Other Books in the Current Controversies Series

Whistleblowers

Anna E. Lindner, Book Editor

Published in 2020 by Greenhaven Publishing, LLC
353 3rd Avenue, Suite 255, New York, NY 10010

First Edition

Articles in Greenhaven Publishing anthologies are often edited for length to meet page
requirements. In addition, original titles of these works are changed to clearly present
the main thesis and to explicitly indicate the author's opinion. Every effort is made to
ensure that Greenhaven Publishing accurately reflects the original intent of the authors.
Every effort has been made to trace the owners of the copyrighted material.

Cover image: Frederick Florin/AFP/Getty Images

Library of Congress Cataloging-in-Publication Data

Names: Lindner, Anna E., editor, compiler.
Title: Whistleblowers / Anna E. Lindner, book editor.
Other titles: Whistle blowers
Description: First edition. | New York : Greenhaven Publishing, 2020. |
  Series: Current controversies | Includes bibliographical references and
  index. | Audience: Grades 9–12.
Identifiers: LCCN 2019000888| ISBN 9781534505308 (library bound) | ISBN
  9781534505315 (pbk.)
Subjects: LCSH: Whistle blowing—Law and legislation—Juvenile literature.
Classification: LCC K1773 .W48 2019 | DDC 342/.068—dc23
LC record available at https://lccn.loc.gov/2019000888

Manufactured in the United States of America

Website: http://greenhavenpublishing.com

Contents

Chapter 1: Is Whistleblowing Inherently Ethical?

Steven Mintz

In this viewpoint, Mintz provides an overview of the controversy over the ethics of whistleblowing. He considers oft-cited arguments from several perspectives, as well as the various aspects of whistleblowing ethics.

Yes: Whistleblowing Is Central to a Strong Society

Barbara Platt

The history of whistleblowing throughout Western history reveals the central role transparency has played in ensuring the strength of societies.

Daniel Hurson

Recent reports of fraud indicate that corruption remains rampant, revealing the ethical necessity of exposing wrongdoing.

No: Whistleblowers Do Not Always
Have the Moral Upper Hand

Steven Mintz

Following the logic of ethics, Mintz exposits the concepts of fairness and morality in the context of whistleblowing.

Chapter 2: Does One's Identity Factor into Whistleblowing?

Yes: Identity Impacts the Results of Whistleblowing Cases

Foreword

"Controversy" is a word that has an undeniably unpleasant connotation. It carries a definite negative charge. Controversy can spoil family gatherings, spread a chill around classroom and campus discussion, inflame public discourse, open raw civic wounds, and lead to the ouster of public officials. We often feel that controversy is almost akin to bad manners, a rude and shocking eruption of that which must not be spoken or thought of in polite, tightly guarded society. To avoid controversy, to quell controversy, is often seen as a public good, a victory for etiquette, perhaps even a moral or ethical imperative.

Yet the studious, deliberate avoidance of controversy is also a whitewashing, a denial, a death threat to democracy. It is a false sterilizing and sanitizing and superficial ordering of the messy, ragged, chaotic, at times ugly processes by which a healthy democracy identifies and confronts challenges, engages in passionate debate about appropriate approaches and solutions, and arrives at something like a consensus and a broadly accepted and supported way forward. Controversy is the megaphone, the speaker's corner, the public square through which the citizenry finds and uses its voice. Controversy is the life's blood of our democracy and absolutely essential to the vibrant health of our society.

Our present age is certainly no stranger to controversy. We are consumed by fierce debates about technology, privacy, political correctness, poverty, violence, crime and policing, guns, immigration, civil and human rights, terrorism, militarism, environmental protection, and gender and racial equality. Loudly competing voices are raised every day, shouting opposing opinions, putting forth competing agendas, and summoning starkly different visions of a utopian or dystopian future. Often these voices attempt to shout the others down; there is precious little listening and considering among the cacophonous din. Yet listening and considering, too, are essential to the health of a democracy. If controversy is democracy's lusty lifeblood, respectful listening and careful thought are its higher faculties, its brain, its conscience.

Current Controversies does not shy away from or attempt to hush the loudly competing voices. It seeks to provide readers with as wide and representative as possible a range of articulate voices on any given controversy of the day, separates each one out to allow it to be heard clearly and fairly, and encourages careful listening to each of these well-crafted, thoughtfully expressed opinions, supplied by some of today's leading academics, thinkers, analysts, politicians, policy makers, economists, activists, change agents, and advocates. Only after listening to a wide range of opinions on an issue, evaluating the strengths and weaknesses of each argument, assessing how well the facts and available evidence mesh with the stated opinions and conclusions, and thoughtfully and critically examining one's own beliefs and conscience can the reader begin to arrive at his or her own conclusions and articulate his or her own stance on the spotlighted controversy.

This process is facilitated and supported in each Current Controversies volume by an introduction and chapter overviews that provide readers with the essential context they need to begin engaging with the spotlighted controversies, with the debates surrounding them, and with their own perhaps shifting or nascent opinions on them. Chapters are organized around several key questions that are answered with diverse opinions representing all points on the political spectrum. In its content, organization, and methodology, readers are encouraged to determine the authors' point of view and purpose, interrogate and analyze the various arguments and their rhetoric and structure, evaluate the arguments' strengths and weaknesses, test their claims against available facts and evidence, judge the validity of the reasoning, and bring into clearer, sharper focus the reader's own beliefs and conclusions and how they may differ from or align with those in the collection or those of classmates.

Research has shown that reading comprehension skills improve dramatically when students are provided with compelling, intriguing, and relevant "discussable" texts. The subject matter of these collections could not be more compelling, intriguing, or urgently relevant to today's students and the world they are poised to inherit. The anthologized articles also provide the basis for stimulating, lively, and passionate classroom debates. Students who are compelled to anticipate objections to their own argument and identify the flaws in those of an opponent read more carefully, think more critically, and steep themselves in relevant context, facts, and information more thoroughly. In short, using discussable text of the kind provided by every single volume in the Current Controversies series encourages close reading, facilitates reading comprehension, fosters research, strengthens critical thinking, and greatly enlivens and energizes classroom discussion and participation. The entire learning process is deepened, extended, and strengthened.

If we are to foster a knowledgeable, responsible, active, and engaged citizenry, we must provide readers with the intellectual, interpretive, and critical-thinking tools and experience necessary to make sense of the world around them and of the all-important debates and arguments that inform it. We must encourage them not to run away from or attempt to quell controversy but to embrace it in a responsible, conscientious, and thoughtful way, to sharpen and strengthen their own informed opinions by listening to and critically analyzing those of others. This series encourages respectful engagement with and analysis of current controversies and competing opinions and fosters a resulting increase in the strength and rigor of one's own opinions and stances. As such, it helps readers assume their rightful place in the public square and provides them with the skills necessary to uphold their awesome responsibility—guaranteeing the continued and future health of a vital, vibrant, and free democracy.

Introduction

> *"Often the best source of information about waste, fraud, and abuse in government is an existing government employee committed to public integrity and willing to speak out."*
>
> *– Former US President Barack Obama*

Whistleblowing is generally understood to be the act of uncovering an instance of fraud, corruption, or other forms of wrongdoing committed by an individual or a corporation. In a democratic society, it is important to have systems by which all citizens, regardless of status, can report illegal activity. Such transparency serves as a check to the power of the wealthy and influential, as well as that of large organizations.

Indeed, whistleblowing has been a part of American democracy since at least 1773, when Benjamin Franklin uncovered a series of confidential letters documenting the illicit actions of a governor. He then informed the public of the deceit, becoming among the first American whistleblowers. Although the United States has the most extensive whistleblower laws in the world, countries across the globe, particularly those with democratic societies, have developed their own protocols and laws to guide whistleblowing. Although this volume focuses primarily on North America, whistleblower laws and practices in the United States often parallel those of other comparable countries.

Keeping the powers-that-be accountable for their actions is generally considered a necessary tenet of the freedom of expression. However, who decides to blow the whistle, as well as how, when, and why the reporting occurs makes whistleblowing a complex issue. Some potential whistleblowers hesitate to come forward, fearing repercussions from their employers or other powerful entities. Others blow the whistle without sufficient evidence or for selfish reasons. A notable example is Edward Snowden, a controversial figure who is both lauded and condemned for uncovering the National Security Agency's (NSA) often-secret inner workings. Recent financial incentives offered by the government, such as those instituted by the Frank-Dodd Act in 2010, further complicate whistleblower cases. Over the last decade, legislation has been passed that significantly increases the governmental incentives offered to those who blow the whistle. The general hope is that by providing financial rewards, corruption and other unwanted behavior will be limited. However, it has also been argued that incentives themselves create corruption among would-be whistleblowers: an unintended but alarming effect.

Investigating fraud or other illegal conduct is never straightforward, and the whistleblower may be caught up in the red tape and power struggles of the situation that go far beyond his or her reach. In addition, legislature can vary between the state and national levels, as well as between different states, making the system even more difficult to navigate. Cases involving fraud and other illegal activities can be drawn-out, multi-faceted, and difficult to conclude. Anyone considering blowing the whistle must be prepared to deal with the legal, social, and financial consequences of involvement with the judicial system, which may not end how one hopes or expects.

In the era of social media and technologies that allow for nearly uninhibited surveillance, questions regarding the ethics of reporting become even more pertinent. The wealth of information available on the internet may make it easier to detect fraud, but it also allows wrongdoing to be perpetrated with ease. Furthermore, although whistleblower laws have been designated to protect a reporter's identity, the internet and other media increase the chance that one's identity—as well as other information—could be leaked to the public, as occurred in the infamous WikiLeaks case. As a result, the possibility of a public scandal adds another layer of complexity to a potential case. Additionally, the ethics of the workplace often come into play: many whistleblowers are employees who expose the wrongdoing perpetrated by their employers. The culture of a whistleblower's workplace can therefore influence the facts, context, and results of a whistleblower case.

Controversy over the viability of whistleblowing as governmental policy has been furiously debated in recent years. Given the fallout that seems to be inevitable in most whistleblower cases, some wonder if incentivizing whistleblowers is the most effective and efficient way to combat corruption within our political and social systems. Whistleblowing by itself cannot possibly address all iterations of corruption, which in most cases is a deeply rooted, systemic problem. However, others have pointed out that whistleblowing is currently the best option we have for uncovering wrongdoing. Until we discover a better way to ensure transparency, they argue, the United States must continue to incentivize the practice and protect those who blow the whistle.

Current Controversies: Whistleblowers investigates the history, practices, and controversies surrounding whistleblowing in North America and beyond. A broad range of politicians, legal experts, scholars, and concerned-citizen bloggers offer their thoughts on the whistleblowing controversy. By reviewing conflicting viewpoints, readers are encouraged to consider the reasons behind every argument before developing a nuanced position on whistleblowing and its social impact.

CHAPTER 1

Is Whistleblowing Inherently Ethical?

Although Many Believe Whistleblowing to Be Ethical, Complications Remain

Steven Mintz

Dr. Steven Mintz is a professor at Orfalea College of Business who runs a philosophical blog on ethics called the Ethics Sage. *He has also published textbooks on ethics within the business world.*

The ethics of whistleblowing is a tricky matter. Whistleblowing brings two moral values, fairness and loyalty, into conflict. Doing what is fair or just (e.g., promoting an employee based on talent alone) often conflicts with showing loyalty (e.g., promoting a longstanding but unskilled employee). Taken to its extreme from a loyalty perspective, whistleblowing may involve agonizing conflicts when, for example, it involves violating the trust of co-workers who have engaged in wrongdoing or jeopardizing one's "team player" status by going against the prevailing winds in an organization that fosters unethical behavior.

From an ethical perspective, while loyalty is an ethical value it never should be placed above one's ethical obligation to act responsibly and be accountability for one's actions including reporting wrongdoing in the best interests of the organization and its stakeholders. Responsible people blow the whistle when they believe more harm than good will occur if the whistleblower stays silent. A virtuous whistleblower acts in an ethical manner if she truly believes a responsibility exists to protect the public interest. Such a person is willing to accept the consequences of her actions—i.e., she is accountable for her actions.

An ethical person is one who possesses strong character traits built on courage and informed by the belief that integrity is the backbone of ethical decision-making. A would-be-whistleblower is willing to stand her ground even in the face of pressure from

"Is Whistle-blowing an Ethical Act Practice?" by Steven Mintz, The Ethics Sage, March 24, 2015. Reprinted by permission.

higher-ups to stay silent. It's not because of the possibility of receiving a whistleblower's award. Instead, the whistleblower believes in principled behavior and leads her life in accordance with ethical values.

But, what if a whistleblower's motive is to gain a financial reward such as is available through whistleblowing complaints under the Federal False Claims Act and Dodd-Frank? Is it still an ethical practice?

The most important consideration in assessing whether a whistleblower acts in an ethical manner is the intention for one's action. Is it to right a wrong? Is it to give voice to one's values in the face of countervailing forces? Or, is the basis for the action the pursuit of self-interests, which may manifest itself in blowing the whistle in order to cash in on the whistleblower award? After all, greed is a powerful motivating force when considering whether to blow the whistle on financial wrongdoing.

While most would agree with the value of reporting wrongdoing and approve of good organizational governance, external contexts can color acceptance and perception. There are elements of chicken-and-egg, as attitudes that are encouraged in the workplace extend to the street—if businesses promoted good corporate governance for all, whistleblowing wouldn't be viewed negatively or as solely the preserve of business or community leaders.

From a personal perspective, it could be argued that it is incongruous for human nature to display loyalty to a bureaucratic organization because it is composed of so many different people. This dehumanizing environment could distort the whistleblower's perception of their relevance within a company or their ability to influence change, thus degrading their sense of responsibility and motivation to report.

As long as the whistleblower is sure that their motivations are sound and that they are confident in the system, they should not hesitate to relay such information and be pleased that they are helping to create a more ethical organization environment for stakeholders, all of whom benefit from the fair treatment, trustworthiness, and responsibility and accountability.

From an organizational perspective, it is important that even if hotlines are in place, the organization should not be complacent when it comes to its usage and communication. If a company doesn't receive many whistleblowing reports, it shouldn't assume that no news is good news.

In addition, if companies don't use the data collected from their reports in a progressive manner (analyzing trends, investigation and resolution, etc.) it negates the benefits of the service considerably. Businesses have a responsibility to the public to act on whistleblowing intelligence or risk adverse consequences. They are additionally accountable to the governing bodies of their sector, such as the SEC, OSHA, EEOC, EPA, and other regulatory agencies.

It might seem obvious to my readers that I believe whistleblowing is an ethical practice. After all, I blog about it all the time. I also am aware that ethics is easier said than done so it is safe to say that individual ethics are born of a culture of ethics. In an organization, this means to establish an ethical tone at the top that filters throughout and sets a standard that is enforced. The worst thing that can happen in an organization is for top management to say they believe in a code of ethics and then violate that very same code when it comes to their individual behavior.

And in a culture of ethics, whistleblowing can come out of the cold.

Whistleblowing Has Long Been a Part of Western Civilization

Barbara Platt

Barbara Platt writes for Marketplace, *a business and economy radio program, and has experience as a digital content manager and an editor.*

Whistleblowers expose frauds and scandals, and have the power to upend a company's bottom line. You don't have to look any further than the recent headlines around Theranos — which was exposed by a whistleblower for defrauding investors, leading the company's value to plummet from billions to zero — to know that reporting misconduct does make a difference.

But what really is the act of whistleblowing? What are the benefits? The risks? And, if you decide to become a whistleblower, will you be protected?

To put it simply, whistleblowing means to report misconduct or illegal activities of a fellow employee, a higher up or an entire company or government agency. A whistleblower is someone who speaks up when he or she sees something that is ethically or legally wrong happening at their workplace.

Whistleblowing goes back in history as far as medieval England, around the seventh century, according to Whistleblowers International. Medieval England is where the phrase "qui tam" originates, which today refers to a whistleblower lawsuit. Qui tam is short for the Latin phrase "qui tam pro domino rege quam pro se ipso in hac parte sequitur," which translates to "he who prosecutes for himself as well as for the king."

The first whistleblower in America was none other than Benjamin Franklin, who in 1773 exposed Thomas Hutchinson, the royally appointed governor of Massachusetts, after he found letters showing the politician was misleading Parliament, advocating for more troops to be sent to the colonies to control and repress people who were revolting against new taxes. This case and similar ones during this time in America laid the groundwork for the whistleblower protection laws we have today.

There are several laws in place today to help protect whistleblowers. One of the most notable is the Whistleblower Protection Act of 1989, which protects federal employees who report misconduct within their agency. There's also the False Claims Act or the "Lincoln Law," which was enacted in 1863 under the Lincoln administration after contractors supplied soldiers with low-quality gear during the Civil War. In a provision under the False Claims Act, aptly titled qui tam, private citizens are allowed to bring a lawsuit against a corporation on behalf of the federal government. The First Amendment also protects public employees from retaliation from government agencies if an employee chooses to speak out against misconduct. There are also many state laws in place to help protect whistleblowers. According to the National Conference of State Legislatures, 34 states in the country have laws on the books.

Despite all the protections that exist, a company can still make it incredibly difficult for a whistleblower once they've come forward. After 26-year-old Tyler Shultz contacted New York state's public health lab to report his former employer, health technology corporation Theranos, for manipulating proficiency lab testing and talked with the *Wall Street Journal*, Theranos retaliated against him. Shultz said that Theranos accused him of leaking trade secrets and violating a confidentiality agreement, and had him followed by a private investigator hired by the company. He and his parents have spent more than $400,000 in legal fees for his whistleblowing actions, despite the fact that the claim he made has turned out to be accurate.

An older yet equally famous whistleblower case is that of Jeffrey Wigand, who in the early 1990s was a senior executive at Brown & Williamson tobacco company. He blew the whistle on the company, telling a grand jury and the media the dark and dirty secrets of Big Tobacco: that using it could lead to serious, life-threatening diseases, that it was very addictive and that the industry knew these facts and were trying to hide them from the public.

While Wigand did not take down the tobacco industry, his information aided in lawsuits that ended up costing the industry hundreds of billions of dollars. His decision to come forward got him an undesirable amount of attention from the media and as well as several lawsuits, not just from his former employer Brown & Williamson, but from many other tobacco giants. However, speaking with the *New York Times* a few years later, Wigand said he did not regret the decision he made to blow the whistle. Today, he lectures on tobacco-related issues around the world and runs a nonprofit he founded called Smoke-Free Kids.

Not every company sees whistleblowers as the enemy. Many companies embrace whistleblowing policies in order to create an honest and open environment and a transparent culture. This pays off, according to the Association of Certified Fraud Examiners, the largest anti-fraud organization in the world. In a 2014 study conducted by the organization, it found that receiving tips on misconduct is the main way that companies detect fraud; it accounted for 42.2 percent. So while being a whistleblower is far from an easy task, it is a vitally important one for both companies and the public good.

In the Current Era of Corruption, Whistleblowing Is Crucial

Daniel Hurson

Over the past forty years, Daniel Hurson has represented many individuals as an attorney and has assisted the Securities and Exchange Commission in developing whistleblower laws.

Of late we have been saturated with reports of discovery of fraud and corruption of one kind of another in all parts of the world, fueled by greed, easy money, lax enforcement, and modern technology run amok—where a bunch of hackers in an overseas internet café, or perhaps even connected to a government or two, can steal our money, stare at us through our own computers, steal our emails, or wipe out our bank accounts. Simultaneously, a different class of criminals—corrupt corporate managers and the political and government figures who enrich each other through bribes for official acts—have dominated international headlines.

The fact is that there now exist multiple fraud schemes operating internationally that seem to confound international law enforcement. Some are enabled by technology, such as internet frauds and cyber-attacks. Some involve the many forms of money-laundering, offshore accounts, straw-entities, and similar frauds. For example, from a recent Transparency International report we learn (perhaps surprisingly) that Canada "is one of the world's most opaque jurisdictions when it comes to ownership of private companies and trusts" which allows anonymous companies and trusts to "hide behind a veil of secrecy, while giving them access to bank accounts and the means to use their illegally obtained wealth in Canada's legal economy." Such individuals use shell companies to buy real estate, driving up prices in Toronto and Vancouver. The same secrecy may be occurring in sales of the new mega-high

"United States: 'Show Me The Money'—Incentivizing Whistleblowers To Report Fraud And Corruption," by Daniel J. Hurson, Mondaq, January 20, 2017. Reprinted by permission.

rise condos in New York City to various wealthy miscreants from around the globe, hidden behind layers of LLC's. The Panama Papers laid bare the staggering amount of wealth being shifted around the globe, much of which may be ill-gotten in one scheme or another.

In like fashion are the numerous massive international bribery and corruption plots that are repeatedly being disclosed, often ensnaring major international companies and their senior executives. In December a South American sports marketing company entered into a deferred prosecution agreement with the Department of Justice admitting its role in a 15-year scheme to pay tens-of-millions of dollars in bribes and kickbacks to a high-ranking FIFA official to secure his support for acquiring the rights to broadcast the four future editions of the FIFA World Cup.

In another New York federal courtroom in December, Odebrecht, Latin America's largest construction company, and its affiliated petrochemical firm Braskem, pled guilty to bribing government officials in a dozen countries. The firms will pay at least $3.5 billion in penalties to authorities in the US, Brazil and Switzerland in the biggest FCPA settlement ever. Odebrecht, which built the Miami International Airport and has operations in 27 countries, was accused of colluding with Petrobras, the Brazilian state-owned oil company, to take more than a billion dollars in kickbacks from the oil company. That case has resulted in 112 convictions of 83 people, and has rocked that country to its core. Odebrecht created a secret internal group officially known as the "Division of Structured Operations," but called the "Department of Bribery" by prosecutors, which "systematically paid hundreds of millions of dollars to corrupt government officials in countries on three continents."

Massive FCPA settlements are becoming almost routine. Teva Pharmaceutical, an Israeli company, paid $519 million in December. Och-Ziff Capital Management Group, a hedge fund, paid $412 million in September. VimpelCom, a Dutch telecom, paid almost $400 million earlier in 2016. Together with Odebrecht/

Braskem at $420 million, these were four of the ten biggest FCPA cases of all time. Not too far behind last year were JP Morgan Chase ($264 million), and Embraer SA ($205 million). In all, 27 companies paid about $2.48 billion in 2016 to resolve FCPA cases, involving millions in bribes spread all around the globe. Many of these cases involved close cooperation between the SEC and DOJ and foreign government enforcement authorities. Long gone are the days when US companies complained that they were being singled out for paying bribes while foreign competitors were never touched. Now, the big money penalties seem more often to be extracted by non-US companies who are within the broad jurisdictional reach of the SEC and/or the DOJ.

In one sense, it is encouraging that so many corrupt fraudsters are getting caught. Of course these cases take years to be investigated, at great cost and effort to the enforcement agencies in multiple countries. There have been tremendous successes brought about by hard work on the part of investigators and prosecutors around the world. But we cannot help but be distressed at the obvious fact that bribery and corruption on an international scale seems to be on the rise, and are taking new and more malicious forms, particularly cyber-crime, with its ominous potential for economic, social, and political upheaval and chaos. The bribes are now in the millions, even billions, and reach into every country on earth. The cyber-attacks are constant, and ingenious. The crooks hide in the shadows of internet cafes and the bright light of boardrooms and computer screens. Billions of corrupt dollars move secretly in wire transfers and between offshore accounts. Can anything be done?

Is the International Response Enough?

What is the international community doing to combat this onslaught? How can law enforcement get the better of such malevolence, ranging from individual hackers and phone frauds to highly organized international corporate bribery involving billions, and everything in between? Fortunately, in recent years there have developed increasingly influential international efforts at curbing bribery. The Organisation for Economic Cooperation and Development (OECD) has undertaken an international effort to combat bribery and corruption of foreign officials. Forty-one countries are parties to its Anti-Bribery Convention, adopted in 1997, a legally binding international agreement, in which the "Parties to the Convention agree to establish the bribery of foreign public officials as a criminal offense under their laws and to investigate, prosecute and sanction this offence."[1]

OECD has an active "Working Group on Bribery" setting global standards for fighting foreign bribery. And as mandated in a recent Working Group report, "The Liability of Legal Persons: A Stocktaking Report," the signing parties, for example, must establish systems of liability of legal persons and to provide that firms found guilty of foreign bribery are subject to "effective, proportionate and dissuasive" sanctions. OECD has issued 195 monitoring reports covering the 41 signatories' foreign bribery laws and enforcement practices and activities, and has issued over 1450 recommendations for anti-bribery law and enforcement, most of which have been fully or partially implemented. Eighteen countries have introduced or strengthened whistleblower protections.

[...]

Disfavor of Anonymous Reporting

The OECD also commented upon the fact that many countries prohibit anonymous reporting, which is a staple of the SEC Whistleblower program. These parties were skeptical about anonymous whistleblowers, assuming they might be filing unreliable or vindictive allegations, and might attract "cranks, timewasters and the querulants."[2] On the other side were countries that support anonymous whistleblowing, especially where it is culturally unsuitable to be a whistleblower, or where "the institutional safeguards are non-existent of too weak to provide adequate protection." Overall, the OECD reported that (as of the 2014 survey) 41% of signatory countries did not allow anonymous whistleblowing.[3]

In my view, anonymous whistleblowing is essential to the success of any whistleblower program. In my practice, virtually all my clients wish to remain anonymous. The reality of whistleblowing is that legal protections against retaliation cannot prevent such reactions by employers and fellow employees. In the case of former employees or third parties who are whistleblowing, which is often the case, forcing them to identify themselves makes little sense, and can only encourage more aggressive retaliation, such as blacklisting the whistleblower in the industry in which he or she has made their living. This kind of retaliation, which I believe is rampant against whistleblowers, can rarely be stopped by lawsuits or other legal means, and is quite difficult to prove in any event. If the anonymous allegations are truly frivolous, the matter will quickly be disposed of. But if whistleblowers are forced to identify themselves, even if promised confidentiality, most will be unwilling to run the risk.[4]

The OECD did come out strongly in support of strict "confidentiality" for whistleblowers, regardless of whether the country's laws provided for anonymous reporting. "Being certain that the information provided remains confidential, along with one's identity, is an essential factor in disclosing wrongdoing. Maintaining confidentiality is the first element of a whistleblower protection system, when this fails, reprisals may ensue." *Id.* But again, in my experience, and given the nature of the modern corporate workplace and the typical path an internal investigation may take after the whistleblower comes forward, it is nearly impossible to insure that the identity of the whistleblower will not become known or at least suspected within the company or organization. The information given, to be effective, must be direct, specific, and credible. It will generally have to be disclosed to numerous legal, management, compliance, and other officials, as well as to regulators. It may have to be disclosed in some form individuals the whistleblower knows to be culpable or antagonistic to him. Throughout all these steps, the likelihood that the identity of the whistleblower will emerge, or be surmised, is very great, regardless of what efforts are made to keep it confidential. This is true even when the whistleblower remains anonymous, but is almost certain to occur when he or she has to identify themselves to their employer. I believe that the OECD, and member countries, must revisit the confidentiality and anonymity issue and strongly consider a system of anonymous reporting such as that employed by the SEC, CFTC, and the DOJ in the United States.

[…]

Offering Awards to Whistleblowers—A Controversial Incentive

The OECD March 2016 Conference took note of the fact that "[c]ountries have recently adopted novel tools, such as monetary incentives for whistleblowers...to promote reporting." It observed that "these efforts can be particularly valuable in countries where the public is generally reluctant to blow the whistle." I am not sure in which countries citizens are eager to blow the whistle, but I do note that the SEC (which does give awards) has, since inception of its program, received tips from 103 countries outside the US. In FY 2016, the SEC received tips from individuals in 67 countries. Many of my clients have come from outside the US. The largest award yet given to an SEC whistleblower, $30 million, went to a foreign-based whistleblower. It would seem that the prospect of a monetary reward incentivizes whistleblowers worldwide, as it should.

But the concept of giving a monetary award does not seem to have caught on in many countries. The United Kingdom is a good example. In FY 1916 it contributed 63 whistleblower tips to the SEC, the third largest of any foreign country. But in the UK itself, the Public Interest Disclosure Act does not provide any reward for whistleblowing. It does provide compensation for retaliation, however. The whistleblower must have a reasonable belief that the disclosure is made in the public interest and meet certain other criteria. It must be made to the employer or to a "prescribed person" such as a regulatory body. There are rewards for "detriment" or "unfair dismissal." There is no cap on compensation, and the law even allows compensation for being denied promotion or even "injury to feelings." In fact, this approach appears to me to be more "whistleblower friendly" than the convoluted and frustrating process of pursuing compensation for retaliation in the US through the OSHA process required by the Sarbanes-Oxley Act or the requirement to file a federal court case under SOX or Dodd-Frank. But the UK law does nothing to encourage a whistleblower to come forward before any retaliation in the hope of obtaining a multi-million dollar award, as the SEC program offers. UK regulators have looked at the possibility of giving awards, but apparently concluded that "reporting wrongdoing should be its own reward." This may be in part why so many SEC tips come in from the UK.

As for the French, they have just enacted a new law on "transparency, anti-corruption and economic modernization" the so-called Sapin II bill. It obligates French companies having 500 or more employees and revenue exceeding 100 million Euros to implement anti-corruption compliance programs consisting of eight concrete measures, including codes of conduct, internal alert systems, and due diligence and risk assessment procedures. It also introduces a French-style deferred prosecution agreement. It strengthens whistleblower protections and sets forth a structured procedure for whistleblowers to raise claims and to protect against retaliation, including financial compensation in the event of litigation. The law makes it a crime (two years' prison and a 30,000 Euro fine) to retaliate against a whistleblower, violate the whistleblower's confidentiality, and interfere with a "public interest" disclosure (something the US should seriously consider).

A new independent institution, the "Defender of Rights" is created with the authority to enforce the law and to grant financial compensation to victimized whistleblowers, including return to their job and preservation of salary. But the worker has to report to the employer first, not to the Rights Defendant, and has to prove they have disclosed the information in "good faith." As with the UK, there are no awards for providing the information. Last year the

SEC got only three tips from France. Several of the biggest FCPA cases have been against French companies (Alstom, $772 million, Total SA $398 million). Maybe the tips from France will increase.

Canada has created a confused system. Whistleblower programs have been created by the Ontario Securities Commission (OSC) and the Autorite des marches financiers (AMF) in Quebec. Whistleblowers meeting certain criteria will be eligible for a monetary reward by the OSC for a breach of Ontario securities law, if they provide meaningful information and the penalties exceed $1 million. The award can range between 5% and 15% of the penalty but is capped at $1.5 million unless the OSC receives more than $10 million, in which case the maximum award can go to $5 million. The program requirements appear to closely follow the SEC and CFTC programs in the United States. Retaliation protection is also similar to US law. But the AMF program does not offer awards, just retaliation protection. That body studied various whistleblower programs in other countries and "concluded that it cannot be established with certainly that financial incentives generate more quality reporting of wrongdoing, and that the key component of any whistleblower program is in fact the protection offered to whistleblowers."[5] Having by now represented many whistleblowers, I must disagree.

Conclusion

International corruption has reached dangerous levels, and law enforcement is only scratching the surface with the prosecutions undertaken and reported to date. Various international bodies and NGO's have done a good job of alerting the world to the extent of these dangers, and have proposed numerous well-founded recommendations, including many to protect whistleblowers. But the will or ability to enforce the various patchwork of laws prohibiting retaliation of whistleblowers leads much to be desired.

The SEC and CFTC whistleblower programs, which provide substantial monetary rewards to whistleblowers, have clearly set the standard for such efforts, although some of the European laws may provide, at least on paper, greater retaliation protections. Moreover, the European programs, by and large, seem to rigidly cling to outmoded concepts prohibiting anonymous reporting and requiring reporting up to potentially corrupt superiors, at the risk of disclosure of the whistleblower's identity. But the awards programs offered by the US enforcement agencies truly provide the *incentive* to whistleblowers initially to come forward, which after-the-fact retaliation protections alone cannot. In contrast, the European programs seem to shun awards, even to a whistleblower who could expose a complex fraud which nets the regulator millions or even billions of dollars in penalties.

As the SEC program in particular continues to turn out huge multimillion dollar payments to even a small and select group of whistleblowers, it will continue to attract quality tips from around the world (its number of tips has increased 40% since the program's inception, and continues to grow). If other nations truly desire to successfully prosecute sophisticated and entrenched international corruption, they must rethink their opposition to making significant awards to whistleblowers who risk their safety, reputation, and careers to uncover and disclose that corruption by the highest levels of corporate and government power.

Notes

1. "*Fighting The Crime of Foreign Bribery—The Anti-Bribery Convention and the OECD Working Group on Bribery.*" OECD, www.oecd.org/corruption/anti-bribery.

2. A "querulant" (as defined by Wikipedia): "In the legal profession and courts, a **querulant** (from the Latin querulus - "complaining") is a person who obsessively feels wronged, particularly about minor causes of action. In particular, the term is used for those who repeatedly petition authorities or pursue legal actions based on manifestly unfounded grounds." While of course none of my clients fit this definition, I am not sure I can say the same for some parties (and their counsel) I have opposed in litigation.

3. In 2014, the Council of Europe published an aggressive set of standards for the protection of whistleblowers. *Protection of Whistleblowers*, Recommendation CM/Rec(2014)7. But, when it came to anonymous reporting, even the Council expressed concerns: "In most legal systems, there is little or no readily available protection for someone who makes a report to a public authority or a disclosure to the public even if it is made honestly, is justified and is reasonable. Accordingly, such reports or disclosures are often made anonymously in the hope that the

source will be protected. However, anonymity raises a host of issues. More often than not, anonymous allegations are assumed to be malicious or are considered to be less credible by those who receive them. Anonymous disclosures can also be much more difficult to investigate and even impossible to remedy. Finally, anonymity is not a guarantee that the source of the information will not be unmasked. Where the person is identified, the fact that they acted anonymously can be seen as a sign of bad faith, further jeopardizing their position. In the worst cases such people forfeit their career. Their plight then attracts media attention, which can only discourage others from sounding the alarm."

4. In the SEC and CFTC programs, the whistleblower eventually does have to confidentially identify herself in order to claim an award. The SEC also cautions whistleblowers that it cannot guarantee confidentiality if the matter goes into litigation, as defendants will have discovery rights to the SEC files. Fortunately, the vast majority of these cases are settled before extensive discovery.

5. *Canadian Securities Law*, Strikeman Elliott, July 15, 2016.

The Ethics of Reporting Wrongdoing Are Often Complicated

Steven Mintz

Dr. Steven Mintz is a professor at Orfalea College of Business who runs a philosophical blog on ethics called the Ethics Sage. *He has also published textbooks on ethics within the business world.*

I have always been intrigued by the philosophy of whistleblowing. Today's blog explores the philosophical underpinnings of whistleblowing as a moral act—one of conscience and not motivated by self-interest.

A broad view of whistleblowing is the disclosure by organization members (former or current) of illegal, immoral, or illegitimate practices under the control of their employers, to persons or organizations that may be able to effect action. This definition includes whistleblowers who use internal channels (e.g., a hot line or ombudsperson) or external channels (e.g., the external auditors or the SEC) to blow the whistle.

There are four elements of the whistleblowing process: the whistleblower, the whistleblowing act or complaint, the party to whom the complaint is made, and the organization against which the complaint is lodged. The act might be labeled as one of "dissidence," somewhat analogous to civil disobedience. It may be seen as disloyal by some but in the public interest by others.

Given that the act of whistleblowing is a personal choice, the key to whether an individual will blow the whistle on wrongdoing is whether the whistleblower perceives organizational policies are designed to encourage moral autonomy, individual responsibility, and organizational support for whistleblowers.

Moral agency is important for the determination of moral behavior and it enables the moral evaluation of the agent's behavior.

"Is Whistleblowing a Moral Act?" by Steven Mintz, The Ethics Sage, July 14, 2015. Reprinted by permission.

The basic characteristic of the philosophical concept of moral agency is autonomy and is viewed in the context of the ability or will to be one's own person. Autonomy plays an important role in conceptions of moral obligation and responsibility.

Autonomous will means to act according to reasons and motives that are taken as one's own and not the product of organizational policies and external forces such as whistleblowing legislation. Autonomous will is the central value in the Kantian tradition of moral philosophy that moral requirements are based on the standard of rationality he called the "Categorical Imperative."

The Categorical Imperative in Kant's ethical system is an unconditional moral law that applies to all rational beings and is independent of any personal motive or desire. Therefore, we could say that even if pressure exists in an organization to not report wrongdoing, a rational, moral person will withstand such pressure, regardless of perceived retaliation, because it is a moral requirement to do so. Kant argued that conformity to the Categorical Imperative, and hence to moral requirements themselves, is essential to rational agency.

Researchers have posed the question of whether workplace whistleblowing is a right, and thus allows for responsible behavior, or whether it is an imposed corporate duty thus resulting in liability of workers. If an organization institutes an internal whistleblowing policy it is because it perceives moral autonomy to be weak. When businesses then implement the policy, it leads to the conclusion that moral autonomy is strong, and employees are expected to blow the whistle. Therefore, if employees do not blow the whistle in accordance with corporate policy they then become liable for not doing so, rendering the policy a tool that controls employee behavior. Responsibility for misdeeds then shifts from the organization to the individual and employees are further stripped of the right to moral autonomy.

Research has shown that what whistleblowers hope and believe their speaking out will achieve, is the correction of what they perceive as an organizational wrongdoing (e.g., fraudulent financial statements). This research also found that not everyone who perceives a wrongdoing, acts upon that perception. In fact, only 42 percent stated they were ready to blow the whistle.

Those who observe wrongdoing but would not do so identify a "retaliatory climate" in their organizations as the primary barrier to blowing the whistle on corporate wrongdoing while those who say they would speak up about it, were confident that they "would not experience managerial retaliation if they blew the whistle." The National Business Ethics Survey found that 46 percent of employees did not blow the whistle for fear of retaliation while 21 percent that reported misconduct said they faced some form of retribution (ERC 2013).

Whistleblowing regulations attempt to protect individuals when they behave responsibly towards society in light of irresponsible behavior by their organizations. This certainly is the motivation for the anti-retaliation provisions of both the Sarbanes-Oxley Act and the Dodd-Frank Financial Reform Act. The acknowledgement of the need for such protection, however, implies that moral agency, autonomy and responsibility are problematic in organizations, or at the very least, that they do not come naturally and are not welcomed when they arrive. When organizations establish an ethical culture and anonymous channels to report wrongdoing, they create an environment that supports whistleblowing and whistleblowers while controlling for possible retaliation.

Whistleblowing always involves an actual or at least declared intention to prevent something bad that would otherwise occur. It always involves information that would not ordinarily be revealed. Most ethicists agree whistleblowing is an ethical action. According to the "standard theory" on whistleblowing, whistleblowing is morally required when it is required at all; people have a moral obligation to prevent serious harm to others if they can do so with little costs to themselves.

The morality of whistleblowing might be viewed from the perspective that corporations have a moral obligation not to harm. De George identifies five criteria when whistleblowing is morally permitted. Briefly, (1) the firm's actions will do serious and considerable harm to others; (2) the whistleblowing act is justifiable once the employee reports it to her immediate supervisor and makes her moral concerns known; (3) absent any action by the supervisor, the employee should take the matter all the way up to the board, if necessary; (4) documented evidence must exist that would convince a reasonable and impartial observer that one's views of the situation is correct and that serious harm may occur; and (5) the employee must reasonably believe that going public will create the necessary change to protect the public and is worth the risk to oneself.

De George's criteria establish the foundation for moral behavior to occur when contemplating whistleblowing. He rejects the position that external whistleblowing is *always* morally justifiable, and also rejects the position that external whistleblowing is *never* morally justifiable. Basically his position is that the whistleblower should have a moral motivation to engage in the act (i.e., to expose unnecessary harm, and illegal or immoral actions).

Ethics and morality go hand in hand. If you face an ethical crisis in the workplace, consider first whether real harm may be done to others if you don't do everything in your power to correct the situation. Then, commit to acting ethically; first considering the consequences of your actions on others including yourself. No one is obligated to take actions that might harm one's own interests. However, our moral obligation to society does obligate us to right a wrong when we see one that has occurred.

To Ensure Security, Certain Intelligence Should Remain Undisclosed

Ross W. Bellaby

Dr. Ross W. Bellaby is a professor at the University of Sheffield who specializes in the ethics of intelligence. He has published several works on ethics.

One of the most important sets of security questions facing modern societies is how much power should be allowed to the intelligence community and how can we ensure that this power is being used correctly. Reports of abuse at detention centres such as Guantanamo Bay and Abu Ghraib, the pervasive growth of technological surveillance and the increased attention on the use of torture for intelligence collection have all highlighted not only the power of the intelligence community but also the likelihood of that power being abused. Information about these events, however, was not revealed by intelligence organisations themselves. Rather the information was either leaked—such as the Snowden and WikiLeaks' revelations—or was the result of a legislative investigation prompted by media claims that took years in writing and was subjected to fierce political wrangling (Baldino, 2010: 62; Finn, 2009; Mazzetti, 2015). The problem is that the intelligence community is allowed and needs a great deal of secrecy in order to carry out its function. Yet, this secrecy can also hide actions that would not necessarily meet the expected ethical or social standards. Moreover, excessively secretive environments actually promote abuses of power by creating an insider mentality that blurs the lines between the need to get results and what is acceptable behaviour towards those on the outside. This has significantly eroded the trust that people have in the intelligence community, and given its

"The ethics of whistleblowing: Creating a new limit on intelligence activity," by Ross W. Bellaby, SAGE Publications, June 7, 2017. http://journals.sagepub.com/doi/full/10.1177/1755088217712069. Licensed under CC BY-ND 4.0.

inherently secretive nature this is something that will be difficult to re-establish. This is not to say, however, that intelligence should be made utterly transparent. Intelligence does play an important and indeed ethical role in protecting the political community, and a key part of that involves using secretive methods to detect, locate and prevent threats. However, it is clear that being allowed carte blanche freedom is not workable.

The problem is that ensuring correct intelligence behaviour is especially difficult, given the need for some secrecy coupled with a complete reliance on existing democratic institutions. By relying on elected officials to act as the main allowed oversight mechanism means simply extending the sphere of secrecy and creating another layer of unobserved actors. In other areas of government, the power of these officials is kept in check through elections whereby the public have the opportunity to examine decisions made and evaluate the consequences. However, with intelligence this ring of protective secrecy surrounds and limits outside observation of those authorising its activity; information is therefore not available to the electorate and so the authorising political community are not kept in check through the normal mechanisms. Furthermore, the current oversight structures are themselves too passive and often rely on the intelligence community to bring things forward for authorisation rather than penetrating their protective shield and investigating their actions. Therefore, this article will argue that whistleblowing can offer an additional form of oversight to act as a release valve by having those on the inside reveal harmful activities and opening them up to greater degrees of external examination. This will include the argument that not only there is a right to whistleblowing, but there also exists a duty to do so when witnessing unjustified harm, and those who fail to act—and blow the whistle—can be blamed and punished as a result. The article will first outline some of the limits of only relying on democratic structures, followed by the argument for a new framework that will outline not only when someone is right to blow the whistle but where they are obliged to.

This framework will then be applied to the Snowden case in order to determine whether he was justified in blowing the whistle and whether the means he used were correct. Finally, it will be applied to the US Senate Select Committee on Intelligence (SSCI) Report "Committee Study of the Central Intelligence Agency's (CIA's) Detention and Interrogation Program" (henceforward referred to as the SSCI Report) to determine whether those involved in the CIA's extraordinary rendition and torture programme had an obligation to reveal the practices used through whistleblowing and whether those who failed to act now face blame. In combination, these criteria will therefore offer both a limitation and licence on whistleblowing in order to provide a reflective and workable additional framework for intelligence oversight.

The Limits of the System

One of the key aspects of intelligence is that it is inherently secretive. It is tasked with finding out what other people wish to keep secret, a battle "between hiders and finders, and the former usually have the easier job" (Jarvis, 2006: 11). This means that its methods, peoples, systems, practices and information are all necessarily kept secret, as letting others know would give them opportunity to undermine the operations. However, too much secrecy can result in practices and systems that are excessively harsh in nature or unequal in application. This is particularly problematic with intelligence because it "possess[es] special powers, such as the ability to interfere with private property or communications, which clearly can limit human rights," and so requires special monitoring by the oversight institutions to ensure that these powers are not misused (Born and Leigh, 2005: 16).

To counter this potential misuse of power democratic structures are proposed as the main checking mechanisms. Indeed, oversight of political power is the mainstay of democratic theory as it places engaged, equal decision-making at its centre, relying on elections and public enquiry as a means of ensuring public engagement and to disinfect any ills of the political elites: "The only stimulus which can keep the ability of the body itself up to a high standard is liability to the watchful criticism of equal ability outside the body" (Hollyer et al., 2007; Mill, 2005: 138; Shapiro, 2003: 200). Therefore, in order to ensure effective intelligence while also having some form of oversight, the current system uses selected elected officials to keep watch, allowing them into the circle of secrecy in order to have access to the relevant information. Extending this circle of secrecy, however, means that there is no one maintaining watch on these oversight actors; they themselves are not open to being held to account as their decision-making is protected. The role of transparency as a means of ensuring correct behaviour by political elites and limiting their potential for abuse of position is undermined at this point. Moreover, offering secrecy to an oversight mechanism that relies on populous support places significant influence on them to carry out popular rather than correct decisions. This is made more problematic in combative electoral systems that encourages "democratic governments" to "emphasise policy decisions that please voters while hiding those which go against the will of the majority," placing pressure to select the correct message and limit contradicting information (Kono, 2006). As former Solicitor-General Erwin Griswold noted, it is apparent "to any person who has considerable experience with classified material that there is massive over-classification and that the principal concern of the classifiers is not with national security, but rather with governmental embarrassment of one sort or another" (Griswold, 1989). Indeed, investigators in the 1970s found that over 90% of information in some departments was inappropriately classified, while following the 9/11 attacks the G.W. Bush administration "encouraged officials to withhold 'sensitive but unclassified information,' which arguably should be disclosed [under the Freedom of Information Act]," as well as lobbying the Homeland Security Act which specifically exempts "critical infrastructure information" from disclosure. This included an expansion of what counted as "sensitive but unclassified" information with officials estimating that "Nearly 75% of all government-held information is 'sensitive but unclassified,'" In 2003, the Bush administration classified over 14 million documents, an increase of 14% on the previous year (Blanton, 2003: 33–35; Joint Security Commission, 1994; Wells, 2004: 1197, 1201, 1202, 1212).

This is then coupled with the distortive effects of having secretive groups that are physically and emotionally closed off from outside influence. Indeed, there is extensive psychological research into the impact of secretive environments on those within a group on how they perceive their own role and those on the outside. The dangers of in-group/out-group differentiation are such that those on the inside lose external reference points that act as a comparative means of measuring one's moral compass, promoting the normalisation and escalation of harmful policies as officers exclude those considered outsiders from their universe of obligation while internal criticism is simultaneously limited as an act of betrayal. The potential for this affect is then heightened as intelligence represents a special "security concern." As a security issue intelligence is raised out of the domestic sphere where political debate is dominant and into the extraordinary-security sphere where the sense of threat and urgency are heightened.

[...]

A Whistleblower's Right and Obligation

The ethical framework proposed sets out a system of criteria for the potential whistleblower to work, though. It establishes the underlying justifying reason from which the obligation to act is drawn from, the authority the whistleblower has to go against the ordinarily imposed authority of their leaders or organisational loyalty, the type of proportional calculations that they should reflect upon as a guide to understanding when whistleblowing is the correct course of action given the surrounding situation, the correct audience to release the information to, and finally, it details the limits of the whistleblower's obligation, arguing that they are relieved of the need to blow the whistle if the personal costs are too great, though they are still left with the right to act.

First, it is important to understand the justifying reason that sits as the core of why the intelligence operative has an obligation to blow the whistle when they see wrongdoing. For whistleblowing, this is drawn from the broad argument that individuals have a duty to prevent harm from being caused to others, and so represents a form of acting in defence of others. At a general level, this can be framed in terms of the "Good Samaritan" argument, whereby "one ought to help, or at least offer to help, those whose welfare is endangered" if there is a minimal cost to oneself (Kleinig, 1976: 385). Indeed, we normally assume that if we can save a human life at minor cost we are obligated to do so. Though Richard DeGeorge (1990) goes further in this argument stating that

> It is not implausible to claim both that we are morally obliged to prevent harm to others at little expense to ourselves, and that we are morally obliged to prevent great harm to a great many others, even at considerable expense to ourselves. (1990: 214)

Indeed, John Rawls' "original position," the classical utilitarian's "sympathetic spectator" or the Golden Rule, each outline how, after we put ourselves in the shoes of those in trouble, we would want the help and creates an obligation to act; or where the need to stop harm being done is seen as being no different to acting to cause others harm.

However, for intelligence there is more than just a general obligation to act but a very specific one that can act as a strong justifying reason for whistleblowing. That is, given that the ethical justification for the use of intelligence is the protection of the political community, when they not only fail to meet this standard but also directly cause the undermining of this, then they fail the very reason for their existence and as such lose their ethical clout. This is not just a case where the intelligence community sees harm being caused to those it is charged with protecting and fails to act but also where the intelligence practice or policy is the actual source of the harm. This means that the obligation to blow the whistle is strong but limited. It is strong in that it requires those who are actively causing harm to have the whistle blown on them, but it is limited to those activities where they are related to the source of the harm. By failing to act on those who could have prevented the harm makes themselves complicit by allowing the harm to continue through their inactivity. It will be argued later, however, that this obligation is not absolute but is mediated in a proportionality calculation whereby the costs to the whistleblower and other, wider costs to society and even the failure of future intelligence missions need to be incorporated into the ethical calculation, mediating the obligation to a right. What this principle does is establish the basis of the obligation, the nature of which in terms of how and when to carry it out is then determined by the additional criteria.

[…]

Conclusion

[…]

There is no culture or framework within intelligence that details exactly when whistleblowing might be used as a means of limiting unjustified harms that certain policies might cause. While in a perfect scenario this might not be necessary, the fundamental flaws of the current oversight mechanisms coupled with the power of intelligence actors and the tendency for overly secretive environments to distort what practices appear appropriate, means that additional safeguards are needed within the system; ones that allow those who already have direct access to intelligence information the guidance to know when they should speak out.

What is key, however, is that proliferate whistleblowing is not a benefit to society or the intelligence community's objective to protect others. Rather, in order for whistleblowing to be justified, the harm being caused by the intelligence community should be such that it cannot be justified, and that the act of whistleblowing is the best remedy. What is innovative about this is that it establishes an obligation to blow the whistle when the intelligence is aware of unjustified harm being caused, but that this obligation is then mediated by the additional proportionality calculations and the different forms the whistleblowing can take. It therefore does allow for some harms as an inherent part of intelligence but recognises that there needs to be limits on this by providing a means for examining when whistleblowing as an act itself is justified through detailing the different expectations to act that actors face; a way of balancing the benefits and harms that whistleblowing can bring; and finally, a more flexible means of proceeding with different whistleblowing forms depending on the circumstances involved.

Certain Conditions Must Be Met in Responsible Whistleblowing

Alix Dunn and Ruth Miller

Alix Dunn co-founded the Engine Room in 2011 and served as Executive Director from 2015 to 2018. Ruth Miller is a writer and researcher based in Oakland, CA. She previously worked as a project manager and UX researcher at the Engine Room.

Large data breaches and leaks now regularly affect even the most seemingly well-guarded organisations and institutions. Over the past five years, a higher volume of data has been released to the public than the previous 50 years put together. This wave of leaks and breaches means that media outlets, the public, and political systems need to decide how best to serve the public interest when data is made available online.

This information can come from many sources:

A data breach is a compromise of security that leads to the accidental or unlawful destruction, loss, alteration, unauthorised disclosure of, or access to protected data. This is often (but not only) as the result of an attack from an outsider. Data dumps from breaches are becoming increasingly common. It can be difficult to distinguish between the two. Examples of data breaches that are assumed to be from outside attacks include things like DC Leaks and the leak of Democratic National Convention emails.

A data leak is a data breach where the source of the data is from someone inside the organisation or institution that has collected that data. This usually takes the form of whistleblowing (the act of telling authorities or the public that someone else is doing something immoral or illegal). A government or private-sector employee who shares data with the public, or a group of individuals that shows that their employer is engaged in what they perceive to be malpractice.

While whistleblowing has led to unprecedented exposure of secret and illegal government surveillance, corporate malfeasance and corruption, there is often little transparency about the decisions that determine when, how, and what data is released to the public.

As a result, there are serious responsible data issues to be grappled with. As with many responsible data grey areas, there are likely few hard and fast rules, but rather questions to be considered and addressed on a contextual basis.

Broadly speaking, responsible data practices for managing and publishing on data leaks from whistleblowers and other sources need to take the following points into consideration (this list is likely not exhaustive!):

- speedy, high quality publication of data leaks relevant to the public interest
- explicit communication about data provenance, governance, and quality taking care to protect sources when relevant
- appropriate planning for preservation and accessibility of large leaks, where relevant (the most obvious being well-organised repositories for preservation and search)
- operational security and residual data that can expose anonymous sources
- explicit principles for responsibly managing, publishing, reporting, and verifying data dumps
- whistleblower policies and media practices that create an enabling environment for whistleblowing and legal protections for whistleblowing

Caring for the People in the Data

Data leaks and whistleblowing inherently requires sharing data without the consent of its creators or owners. In fact, in many cases, data owners are often the target of data leaks. However, owners of the data are unlikely to be the only people reflected in a dataset that hasn't been treated in advance.

Being incidentally included in a particular dataset can have damaging consequences. For example, this summer, WikiLeaks published personally identifiable information of women in Turkey. They appear to have been included in what was thought to have been emails related to President Erdogan. As technosociologist and scholar Zeynep Tufekci wrote at the time, there were serious consequences of this release.

> "I hope that people remember this story when they report about a country without checking with anyone who speaks the language; when they support unaccountable, massive, unfiltered leaks without teaming up with responsible parties like journalists and ethical activists; and when they wonder why so many people around the world are wary of 'internet freedom' when it can mean indiscriminate victimization and senseless violations of privacy."

The responsible approach to dealing with this data would have been to work to verify the data prior to publishing it online, redacting it to ensure that no sensitive data was included, and establishing that the data was indeed an issue of public interest. Given the size and scale of the data, this is harder than it might sound. And in this case, it was made more difficult by language barriers and lack of adequate context to understand the contents of the leak, prior to it being made available online.

As with all responsible data issues—context is queen. In the case of data leaks, the diverse number of actors and incentives in the chain of data handling make understanding and decision-making in diverse contexts challenging.

Data Leaks and Whistleblowing Best Practices

With the advent of high profile whistleblowers, much has been written and done to ensure the safety of those carrying out the act of whistleblowing, both in terms of behavioural best practices, legislative protections, and ensuring that technical best practices are possible via platforms like Secure Drop and GlobaLeaks.

But there are others who need to make important decisions about data leaks: publishers and consumers of the data.

Potential users might include journalists (those working within a newsroom, and freelancers), students, researchers, activists, academics, data scientists, and more. The field of journalism is established enough to have various codes of ethics, dependent upon the newsroom or the particular union, but as a younger field, data science lacks this, as identified by Nathaniel Poor in this case study contemplating the use of hacked data in academia:

> "Journalists use data and information in circumstances where authorities and significant portions of the public don't want the data released, such as with WikiLeaks, and Edward Snowden... However, journalists also have robust professional norms and well-established ethics codes that the relatively young field of data science lacks. Although cases like Snowden are contentious, there is widespread acceptance that journalists have some responsibility to the public good which gives them latitude for professional judgment. Without that history, establishing a peer-group consensus and public goodwill about the right action in data science research is a challenge."

A number of efforts have been made to introduce ethics into data science curricula—which addresses part, but not all, of the problem. Not all of the potential users or even hosters of the data, will identify as a "journalist" or a "data scientist." If data is made available through whistleblowing, perhaps different contextual considerations will apply, though lessons can definitely be learned from other, related sectors.

Calls have long been made for data journalists to consider their ethical responsibilities prior to publishing. Writing about the use of big data by academic researchers, Boyd and Crawford write: "it is unethical for researchers to justify their actions as ethical simply because the data is accessible."

This mantra might well apply to anyone who is thinking of using, or hosting, leaked data—so, what questions should they ask before using that data? Are there red lines that we should never cross, on both the side of the source and the data user—like data on individuals' bank account numbers, health status, sexual orientation, to name just a few. Might it be possible to agree upon a few, shared lines that don't get crossed, even in leaks?

Once someone decides to work with data made available through whistleblowing, what responsible data approaches can they take to ensure that no further harm comes to people reflected in that data set? This might involve taking steps to verify the data and making this process transparent, to ensure that others understand where it came from and what the data represents (and doesn't represent)—or redacting versions of a dataset before publishing it publicly.

Transparency, Privacy, and Protection

Looking at past examples, the approach of radical transparency rarely seems to be the most responsible approach for working with or dealing with data that has been made available through whistleblowing.

Alex Howard and John Wonderlich of the Sunlight Foundation write:

> "Weaponized transparency of private data of people in democratic institutions by unaccountable entities is destructive to our political norms, and to an open, discursive politics.... In every case, for every person described in the data, there's a public interest balancing test that includes foreseeable harms."

From a responsible data approach, those "foreseeable harms" are exactly what need to be outlined in advance and transparently considered. This might well end up being a controversial topic – as with many responsible data issues, things are rarely black and white.

The team behind the Panama Papers decided not to publish their original source documents, with ICIJ director Gerard Ryle quoted in WIRED as saying "We're not WikiLeaks. We're trying to show that journalism can be done responsibly." Discussion on the Responsible Data mailing list revealed multiple perspectives on the issue. Some thought that full transparency of the source documents would have been a better decision, while to others trusted that the team had responsibly taken the decision not to publish for a reason.

Ultimately, as Howard and Wonderlich also outline: protecting the privacy of individuals reflected in data that has been made available through whistleblowing should be of utmost importance.

Trust and Responsibility

Ultimately, what underlines many of these concerns is trust. For the whistleblower releasing information, it is critical to ensure trust in a secure process of putting those leaks to use. It requires a great deal of faith to ask someone whose trust has been betrayed by an institution to then place it within journalists, researchers or activists who they might not personally know.

For a media outlet reporting on data leaks or data breaches of unknown provenance, responsibility is key. Beyond this, individuals need to think carefully about their responsibilities when using and accessing the data, and making it available for others to use in the future.

- What can we do as a community to encourage transparent, explicit communications around those decisions?
- To make it easier for a whistleblower to trust that transparent and responsible processes will be followed, with a duty of care towards both the public interest, and the rights of the people reflected in the data?
- What are ethical ways of reporting on data leaks whose provenance is unknown, or whose provenance is known to be from dubious actors using dubious tactics?
- How can media effectively make decisions and communicate those decisions to its consumers when reporting on data leaks and using them in their reporting?

CHAPTER 2

Does One's Identity Factor into Whistleblowing?

Balancing the Need for Anonymity with the Importance of Accountability

Susie Choi

Susie Choi is an undergraduate at Duke University who studies computer science.

Whistleblowing protections, crowdsourcing, anonymous voting processes, and even Glassdoor reviews—anonymous speech may take many forms in organizations.

As well-established and valued as these anonymous feedback mechanisms may be, anonymous speech becomes a paradoxical idea when one considers how to construct a more open organization. While an inability to discern speaker identity seems non-transparent, an opportunity for anonymity may actually help achieve a *more inclusive and meritocratic* environment.

But before allowing outlets for anonymous speech to propagate, however, leaders of an organization should carefully reflect on whether an organization's "closed" practices make anonymity the unavoidable alternative to free, non-anonymous expression. Though some assurance of anonymity is necessary in a few sensitive and exceptional scenarios, dependence on anonymous feedback channels within an organization may stunt the normalization of a culture that encourages diversity and community.

The Benefits of Anonymity

In the case of *Talley v. California (1960)*, the Supreme Court voided a city ordinance prohibiting the anonymous distribution of handbills, asserting that "there can be no doubt that such an identification requirement would tend to restrict freedom to distribute information and thereby freedom of expression." Our judicial system has legitimized the notion that the protection of anonymity facilitates the expression of otherwise unspoken ideas. A quick scroll through any subreddit exemplifies what the Court has codified: anonymity can foster risk-taking creativity and the inclusion and support of marginalized voices. Anonymity empowers individuals by granting them the safety to speak without detriment to their reputations or, more importantly, their physical selves.

For example, an anonymous suggestion program to garner ideas from members or employees in an organization may strengthen inclusivity and enhance the diversity of suggestions the organization receives. It would also make for a more meritocratic decision-making process, as anonymity would ensure that the quality of the articulated idea, rather than the rank and reputation of the articulator, is what's under evaluation. Allowing members to anonymously vote for anonymously-submitted ideas would help curb the influence of office politics in decisions affecting the organization's growth.

The Harmful Consequences of Anonymity

Yet anonymity and the open value of *accountability* may come into conflict with one another. For instance, when establishing anonymous programs to drive greater diversity and more meritocratic evaluation of ideas, organizations may need to sacrifice the ability to hold speakers accountable for the opinions they express.

Reliance on anonymous speech for serious organizational decision-making may also contribute to complacency in an organizational culture that falls short of openness. Outlets for anonymous speech may be as similar to open as crowdsourcing is—or rather, is not. Like efforts to crowdsource creative ideas, anonymous suggestion programs may create an organizational environment in which diverse perspectives are only valued when an organization's leaders find it convenient to take advantage of members' ideas.

A similar concern holds for anonymous whistleblowing or concern submission. Though anonymity is important for sexual harassment and assault reporting, regularly redirecting member concerns and frustrations to a "complaints box" makes it more difficult for members to hold their organization's leaders accountable for acting on concerns. It may also hinder intra-organizational support networks and advocacy groups from forming around shared concerns, as members would have difficulty identifying others with similar experiences. For example, many working mothers might anonymously submit requests for a lactation room in their workplace, then falsely attribute a lack of action from leaders to a lack of similar concerns from others.

An Anonymity Checklist

Organizations in which anonymous speech is the primary mode of communication, like subreddits, have generated innovative works and thought-provoking discourse. These anonymous networks call attention to the potential for anonymity to help organizations pursue open values of diversity and meritocracy. Organizations in which anonymous speech is *not* the main form of communication should acknowledge the strengths of anonymous speech, but carefully consider whether anonymity is the wisest means to the goal of sustainable openness.

Leaders may find reflecting on the following questions useful prior to establishing outlets for anonymous feedback within their organizations:

- *Availability of additional communication mechanisms*: Rather than investing time and resources into establishing a new, anonymous channel for communication, can the culture or structure of existing avenues of communication be reconfigured to achieve the same goal? This question echoes the open source affinity toward realigning, rather than reinventing, the wheel.
- *Failure of other communication avenues*: How and why is the organization ill-equipped to handle the sensitive issue/

situation at hand through conventional (i.e. non-anonymous) means of communication?

- *Consequences of anonymity:* If implemented, could the anonymous mechanism stifle the normalization of face-to-face discourse about issues important to the organization's growth? If so, how can leaders ensure that members consider the anonymous communication channel a "last resort," without undermining the legitimacy of the anonymous system?

- *Designing the anonymous communication channel:* How can accountability be promoted in anonymous communication without the ability to determine the identity of speakers?

- *Long-term considerations:* Is the anonymous feedback mechanism sustainable, or a temporary solution to a larger organizational issue? If the latter, is launching a campaign to address overarching problems with the organization's communication culture feasible?

These five points build off of one another to help leaders recognize the tradeoffs involved in legitimizing anonymity within their organization. Careful deliberation on these questions may help prevent outlets for anonymous speech from leading to a dangerous sense of complacency with a non-inclusive organizational structure.

When Blowing the Whistle, Gender Matters

Linda Hunt

Dr. Linda Hunt is a professor in the School of Business and Management at Azusa Pacific University who utilizes a gendered lens in her research on business. Her interests revolve around human resource development, strategic planning, and business management.

Women are gaining more notoriety for coming forward and dealing with tough ethical issues in the workplace. At the heart of the concern is whether this is a gender issue. The motivation may be different for women in making the decision to come forward, than for men. Women such as Sherron Watkins have gained fame for stepping forward. Watkins is credited with exposing Enron. Women face unique repercussions and are often more hesitant to bring wrongdoing to the surface. "A combination of idealism, altruism, and concern that what is going on is hurting others prompts women who do not want to make a fuss or be in the limelight to sometimes become reluctant whistleblowers." This paper will explore the unique challenges that women whistleblowers face.

Findings

The term whistleblowing has been around for many years. One of the early federal laws enacted to protect whistleblowers came in 1972 under the Water Pollution Control Act. This act was formulated as a protection to employees against retaliation for coming forward with damaging information. In the mid-eighties several more whistleblower protection laws were enacted. They too were designed to protect employees from retaliation. There are many laws today to protect employees who come forward

"The Challenges Women Whistleblowers Face," by Linda Hunt, Canadian Center of Science and Education, April 2010. http://citeseerx.ist.psu.edu/viewdoc/download?doi=10.1.1.665.5999&rep=rep1&type=pdf. Licensed under CC BY 4.0 International.

with information and most organizations have their own internal policies with the same intentions.

For those that come forward, their life and career are never the same. While laws and polices have the best intentions to protect, people are going to act upon their own accord. Often there is an undercurrent in the environment that makes it very difficult for the whistleblower to remain in the organization. It is a life-changing experience for most whistleblowers. Cynthia Cooper, the corporate whistleblower at the heart of the WorldCom scandal states that being a whistleblower was nothing she had envisioned or hoped to have been. The journey of a corporate whistleblower and a women whistleblower is not an easy road to go down. How does social status affect this issue? Social status in the workplace is about, equality, organizational power and position. When women step out of their perceived social status, retaliation can be the consequence.

Regardless of gender or who is blowing the whistle, the concept is the same. To better understand the concept, it makes sense to explore a couple of definitions. In her article *Encouraging Internal Whistleblowing in Organizations*, Lilanthi Ravishankar (2003, p. 1) defines whistleblowing as "employees who bring wrongdoing at their own organizations to the attention of superiors." That is a simple concept but since there are often legal complications that go along with whistleblowing it is prudent to look at another more descript definition.

Roberta Johnson (2002) defines whistleblowing as:

> an act with these four components; one, an individual acts with the intention of making information public; two, the information is conveyed to parties outside the organization who make it public and part of the public record; three, the information has to do with possible or actual nontrivial wrongdoing in an organization; four, the person exposing the information is not a journalist or ordinary citizen but, a member or former member of the organization (p.3-4).

Nick Perry (1998, p. 235) has a more simplified definition: "Whistleblowers are defined as insiders who go public." It is important to understand that whistleblowing has huge ramifications. Going public with information that will forever change the organization, and likely their relationship with that organization, is a hard decision to make. There is the irrevocable damage to the company and the individual employee. The stress can jeopardize health and family relationships. According to Alford, most whistleblowers are never the same; they suffer a career loss and often loss of their family and relationships. We are taught to be loyal, and breaking that loyalty to do what is perceived is right is often a tough ethic quandary to face, especially for women.

As more women are climbing the corporate ladders and become part of the executive leadership, we are seeing more women in whistleblower situations. As we observe more women in these roles, their decision making and ethics are being scrutinized. Women whistleblowers gained notoriety in December of 2002, when *Time* magazine named the persons of the year, three corporate women whistleblowers.

The *Time* magazine cover in December 2002 featured three prominent whistleblowers: Cynthia Cooper of WorldCom, Colleen Rowley of the FBI, and Sherron Watkins of Enron. These were three women who did the extraordinary thing, by all coming forward to report corporate wrongdoing. They were chosen as persons of the year because they were considered brave role models that were willing to stand for what was right. "The truest of true believers is more like it, ever faithful to the idea that where they worked was place that served the wider world in some important way" (Lacayo & Ripley, 2002, p. 2).

There is a lot of discussion on whether there is a gender component in who is the likelier whistleblower, a man or a woman? The debate is about which sex is more ethical. Some of the most famous corporate scandals can be attributed to men. This may be because fewer women were formerly in the corporate executive roles. Examples are the Ford Pinto disaster and the Dow-Corning toxic breast implants. Because women have just gained more corporate influence over the last decade, it may be too soon to tell if they will make the same type of ethical blunders as did their male counterparts.

There are gender differences which effect decision making and the willingness to come forward to report wrongdoing. One of the differences stems from the theory that women are not part of the male network sometimes called the boys club. Part of the gender thinking difference goes back to lessons learned in childhood. According to Pomeroy winning is what boys are taught, while girls are taught to be nice and play fair. Men and women are raised with a different value system. According to Glaser (2008, p. 1), "As young boys, men jockey for position in the playground and learn to give and take orders." She says that "if boys don't like the rule, they leave the game. Girls on the other hand, play in leaderless groups, not hierarchies, and choose games with far fewer rules." The inference is that if women don't think the rules are just and right, they won't play the game. The gender issue is about the conditioning we learned as children, suggesting that women may be more likely whistleblowers because of lessons learned in childhood games.

Reflecting on our own childhood, it would seem that this theory hits home. Often girls are scolded for not sharing enough and not playing nice, while for boys it is more acceptable to not play nice so long as they win. The influence of the informal men's club that women are often not a part of can be observed in many corporate environments. When a female is the whistleblower, she is considered insubordinate, while males are praised for this same action. If Rappeport has it right, this indicates a definite difference for a woman whistleblower in how they are viewed within their own organization.

Women also have their own networks. While women for the most part desire to be an insider in the boy's club, men do not strive to be included in the women's network. This may also go back to childhood learning. It seems common for a girl to be a tom-boy or one of the guys, but it is uncommon for a boy to be one of the girls. According to Andre and Velasquez women identify with the comradery of relationships and maintaining these relationships can be critically important. This would give credence to the theory that woman who have built these network relationships, would be reluctant to come forward to report wrongdoing. Choosing loyalties is a very hard thing to do, when faced with discovering business improprieties. Cynthia Cooper, the WorldCom executive, sums up best "How many people have looked out this window with fear and anxiety?" (Cooper, 2008, p. 334). Women often have a lot of fear and anxiety about whistleblowing. Some believe it is because of the gender differences and others believe it is because women have more to risk. Social status is a key factor, as there is often an imbalance of power in male dominated organizations. According to Rehg, Miceli, Near and Van Scooter, for women in supervisory positions in organizations dominated by males there is a social expectation of acquiescence. When a female becomes a whistleblower, she is seen as a threat to the social norm.

Fred Alford states that women are often more tied to family than to their organization, which makes them more likely to come forward in the face of wrongdoing. Alford also brings up a good point in saying that because women are not part of the men's network; their outsider status gives them less to risk. They are not risking relationships, as they may not feel included in those relationships.

Another theory is that women are actually more likely to blow the whistle because they are not as entrenched in the organization as men are. According to Lacayo and Ripley, gender does play a role and often these women feel less loyalty because they are viewed as outsiders. Allan Rapperpot states that studies indicate that women place a higher value on honesty than do men. In any case women seem to be getting all the attention for being whistleblowers. Men are still blowing the whistle but getting less attention. It is the type of attention that no one seeks or wants regardless of gender. Doing the right thing and the ethical thing has many long lasting repercussions. The reason a women may decide to come forward may be different than a man, but in both cases those that come forward and make the hard decision to do so, should be honored.

No matter the gender of the whistleblower, retaliation is almost always a given. According to Alford, although there are laws to protect victims from retaliation most do experience some form of retaliation and are sufficiently damaged by the experience. Sherron Watkins, credited as the whistleblower in the Enron scandal, was ignored after she came forward, and given no important projects or tasks for almost one year. Watkins eventually left the company. Retaliation can be done in blatant ways or in less obvious ways that are hard to measure or prove.

Marcia Miceli co-authored a study conducted on a US Airforce base that tackled how women experienced retaliation. The research by Rehg, Miceli, Near and Van Scooter, supports that females are more often victims of retaliation than their male counterparts. Male whistleblowers experienced less retaliation than females. Their research is also based on *Social role theory* which is about power, social influences and those effects on gender. It is the retaliation that women have the highest anxiety over. According to the Institute for Operations Research and the Management Sciences, women do experience more retaliation than men. This information was obtained as a result of several surveys taken. Often there is a loss of power, verbal harassment and a feeling like big brother is watching. It is no surprise that women are often reluctant to step forward and risk their careers to reveal critical information. Again for women it is often about going against the social norm and the consequences that may follow.

To truly understand the unique challenges that women whistleblowers face, careful consideration must be given to the issue of retaliation. It appears that it is the retaliation factor that looms for most women as the critical issue in coming forward. Stepping forward can be an agonizing and painful process. According to the Institute of Operations Research and the Management Sciences

(2008), "The levels of retaliation as perceived by the woman we surveyed were greater than those perceived by men." The best way to fully illustrate the fear factor and of retaliation for women, is to explore some real cases of real women who experienced retaliation.

Laura Bastion was a Department of Defense employee working as a child physiologist assigned in Europe. She was there to carry out a mandate that would ensure that all military personal with special needs children would be afforded the educational programs necessary to assist them in reaching their full potential. According to Alford the problem was that there were too many children to evaluate and she was ineffective at carrying out the mandated task. She wrote a report that indicated what the road blocks were, and it was not well received by her supervisor or the Pentagon. She told the truth, she laid out the issues; she stepped out of the social status level that was acceptable.

The retaliation that she experienced was to have her office relocated to the broom closet in the basement. Next she was asked to undergo a psychological evaluation. She was assigned to a new supervisor whose job seemed to be to watch her and write her up. Several negative performance evaluations followed, and she was pressured to resign her position. The Pentagon looked the other way while the retaliation was going on. But it doesn't end here for Laura Bastion. Laura was obviously a fighter, and believed in standing up for the truth and what is right, or she wouldn't have found herself in this situation.

She took her case to the federal courts for resolution and justice. Laura lost her appeal, but the appeal cost her one hundred thousand dollars. Even thought there are laws to protect whistleblowers from retaliation, the retaliation does become a harsh reality for some. According to Glazer (1998, p. 66), "the legal process is slow and expensive, and it is difficult to obtain remedy for retaliation in the courts." When the victims of retaliation are women, other woman become wearier of standing up for what is right; this is due in part to social conditioning.

Grace Pierce was a research physician who was hired by Ortho Pharmaceutical to do research on an emerging drug called Loperamide. Her job was to determine the safety and recommend the drug for approval. Loperamide was in a liquid form and was used to treat acute diarrhea, which meant that children would be consumers of the final product. The drug had a high concentration of saccharin, which was used to masque the unpleasant flavor.

Grace Pierce headed a research team where she was the only physician. The drug's high saccharin content bothered Pierce because saccharin was a known carcinogenic. She stood up against her team when the recommendation was made to accept the high saccharin content. According to Glazer, the retaliation that Grace Pierce suffered was in the form of having her integrity questioned and being falsely accused of misappropriation of funds.

Pierce ultimately resigned under the unpleasant circumstances. Like Laura Bastion, she also would attempt to take her case through the courts. She also lost her case. Pierce was a notable physician that formerly held positions of honor and respect. She resigned under a cloud of shame and it was difficult for her to maintain her career.

It is likely that as a woman, she overcame many obstacles to become a physician. Women have an uphill road in attaining equal respect in business. It is harder for a woman, once brought down, to ever climb the corporate ladder again. Emotionally, women do not rebound as easily as their male counterparts.

Grace Pierce saw her career destroyed because she stood up and would not allow a cancer-causing drug to be approved for consumption. There is a lack of a support system for women that have become whistleblowers. The courts often fail to support them. Women are often perceived as outsiders, which puts them in the unique situation of having no support from their former colleagues. So for a woman the challenge in being a whistleblower is not only the retaliation but often the isolation.

Conclusion

Becoming a whistleblower was not a premeditated act for any of the women profiled by *Time* magazine; Cynthia Cooper of WorldCom, Colleen Rowley of the FBI, or Sherron Watkins of Enron. It was not the goal of Laura Bastion or Grace Pierce. These are all women who came forward with information because their ethics and values told them it was the right thing to do. According to Pomeroy women do approach ethical concerns in a different manner then men, and that may explain why there have been so many women whistleblowers making the news lately.

What is different for women that come forward is the level of retaliation and the lack of support. According to the Institute of Operations Research and the Management Sciences, women do feel higher levels of retaliation, a lack of support and no matter what level of power the woman had, she still had no support. The authors also note that the wrong-doer power may have an influence over the women's lower power. Social status in an organizational context is about power level and the expectation for that power level. In most all of the cases profiled in this paper, the wrong-doers happened to have been males, so the gender issue becomes more important. Women are often in lower power level positions, so gender and social equality become an issue. The unique challenge that a woman whistleblower faces is in being the outsider blowing the whistle. According to Lacayo and Ripley, gender does play a role and often these women feel less loyalty because they are viewed as outsiders. Women will continue to blow the whistle and report wrong-doing no matter what the consequences are. However when their actions are perceived as not typical for their social status, retaliation is generally the consequence. Social status plays a significant role in the reason women become whistleblowers and the related consequences. Perception and social conditioning of social norms of women's position and power in the workplace will not change easily. Cynthia Cooper's advice to whistleblowers is this "educate yourself about what may happen once you come forward, know who you are at your core, avoid looking to others for self-worth, and move your life in a different direction (Cooper, 2008, p. 314)." While there may be unique challenges for women whistleblowers, knowing those challenges and being prepared for the major changes that will occur is the best recommendation.

Most Whistleblowers Experience Retaliation

Patricia A. Patrick

Dr. Patricia A. Patrick is an associate professor at the Shippensburg University of Pennsylvania who specializes in auditing and forensic accounting.

You might one day need to be a whistleblower. Be forewarned: Your personal and professional lives will suffer. New research on state whistleblower lawsuits shows it's likely you'll be fired and will lose your case. But then, doing the right thing never meant that right things would happen to you.

Imagine this scenario: A government contractor is overcharging your state government agency for goods and services. You know this because you once worked in the billing department of the contractor. You report this to your supervisor who terminates you shortly afterward. So, you file a complaint with the Florida Commission on Human Relations (FCHR), which reinstates you to your position. Your former employer takes the matter to court under Florida's whistleblowing law and has you removed again. The court overturns the FCHR's decision because the whistle-blower law requires a complainant to file within 60 days of the alleged incident and you filed more than 100 days later. Also, the FCHR didn't have jurisdiction to hear your case. Once again, you're out of a job.

My sample of state-level cases shows that outcomes such as this aren't unusual in whistleblower cases filed in American states.

Would-be whistleblowers might wonder if it's worth it, yet many continue to report wrongdoing. Most recently, Amy Stoupe, CFE, the 2010 ACFE Sentinel Award recipient, blew the whistle.

Others who did the right thing include Cynthia Cooper, CFE; Sherron Watkins; Pamela Meyer Davis; Bunny Greenhouse; Marta

"Be Prepared Before You Blow the Whistle," by Patricia A. Patrick, Association of Certified Fraud Examiners, October 2010. Reprinted by permission.

Andreasen; Dr. David J. Graham; and William Sanjour. Of course, all paid a high price to come forward.

As CFEs, we might find it necessary to report wrongdoing, but we should proceed with caution before blowing the whistle. My review of state-level lawsuits suggests that being entitled to protection under a state whistleblower statute and receiving that protection can be two different matters.

State Whistleblowing Laws

All the US states have laws to protect public employees from retaliation. Most of the state whistleblowing laws were enacted to encourage public employees to report fraud, waste, and abuse in government agencies. Some laws protect only public employees; others include government contractors and private-sector employees.

Most of the states also have laws covering private-sector employees. However, many of these laws protect reports involving workplace safety. They were enacted decades ago to protect employees from retaliation when reporting occupational safety issues. Public and private employees can use them, but they might not apply to all situations. Over the years, reporting in other specific situations has been protected.

Many states enacted anti-retaliation clauses for specific claims or industries. For example, Rhode Island has anti-retaliation clauses in statutes pertaining to gaming, nursing homes, health-care facilities, nonprofit hospitals, insurance fraud, health maintenance organizations; and asbestos abatement. Anti-retaliation clauses are designed to protect public and private employees working in specific cases.

The Essence of Blowing That Whistle

Whistleblowing, as it relates to fraud, is the act of reporting fraud, waste, and abuse. Reporting any act of wrongdoing is considered whistleblowing, regardless if it's reported by a public or private employee or to persons inside or outside of the victim organization.

Anyone can report wrongdoing, but the level of protection an employee will receive will differ depending on whether they're public or private, to whom they report, the manner in which they report, the type of wrongdoing they report, and the law under which they report.

Take the Texas Whistle-blower Act, for example. It protects public employees from retaliation who report violations of law to appropriate law enforcement agencies, providing the employee files a grievance within 90 days of when the employer's adverse employment action occurred or was discovered by the employee. The employee must initiate action under the grievance or appeal process of the governmental employer before filing a lawsuit.

The employee must also report the violation in good faith, prove the retaliation is the result of the whistleblowing, and identify the laws violated and the persons engaged in the violations. Employees can be compensated for their losses, but the entity can defend itself by asserting its actions were unrelated to the whistle-blowing. This is an affirmative defense that can be asserted by any employer. Employers using an affirmative defense will admit they took the adverse personnel action but claim the action was due to events independent of the whistleblowing.

If you find Texas' Whistle-blowing Law daunting, you're probably not alone. My review of state-level lawsuits filed by whistleblowers shows that it's difficult to receive protection under many of the state laws.

Research Method

I selected a random sample of lawsuits from the statewide cases reported in the LexisNexis database between 1994 and 2009. I keyed in the search term "whistleblower" and found 380 cases involving whistleblowers who sued their employers for alleged retaliation following the reporting of a wrongful act.

I stratified the lawsuits chronologically by state and selected every fourth case to obtain a random sample of 95 cases. I conducted a content analysis of each case to identify: 1) the type of retaliation taken against the whistleblower 2) the type of wrongdoing reported 3) the public policy issued 4) the outcome for the whistleblower 5) the reason the whistleblower won/lost the lawsuit 6) whether the whistleblower was a public servant 7) the law used to file the case.

Most Whistleblowers Are Fired

Seventy-four percent of the whistleblowers in my review were terminated. Another 6 percent were suspended and 5 percent were transferred against their wishes. The remaining 15 percent were given poor evaluations, demoted or harassed. The results indicate that retaliation occurs, although this review can't determine how often.

Approximately 60 percent of the lawsuits were filed in the past 10 years; however, it's impossible to say why employees are increasingly turning to the courts to solve their problems. Perhaps employees are reporting wrongful acts more frequently and filing more frivolous lawsuits. It's also possible that employers are committing more acts of wrongdoing and retaliating more often. Then again, it's possible the rise is due to the increasingly litigious nature of American society.

The whistleblowers in this sample didn't fare well in their lawsuits. Fifty-five percent lost their cases. Fourteen percent lost because they failed to prove their cases. Eleven percent failed to prove a causal connection between the alleged retaliation and the whistleblowing. Only 22 percent won their lawsuits. Of these, 2 percent were reinstated to their old jobs and 8 percent won damage awards. The remaining 23 percent of the cases were remanded for a new trial.

To prevail, employees will probably have to link their whistle-blowing to the retaliation. This can be difficult for employees having problems in the workplace because employers will claim their adverse personnel actions were based on the employees' poor performances—not the employees' decisions to blow the whistle. It's especially easy for employers to assert this claim if the person who conducted the retaliation claims no knowledge of the whistle-blowing.

Get Technicalities Correct

Twenty-two percent of the whistleblowers lost because they didn't comply with some technicality in the laws. As discussed previously, the laws are very specific on how whistleblowers must report the wrongdoing. Failing to comply with any aspect of the law will result in a loss of protection.

Six percent of the employees lost because they failed to exhaust all their internal remedies before reporting their concerns externally. Many laws require the employee to report internally first to give the employer an opportunity to correct the matter. This minimizes the potentially devastating impact that public reports can have on organizations when the claims don't have merit or could be handled more effectively internally. Internal reports can also allow the employer to conceal the unlawful activity, if they are so inclined.

Another 5 percent lost because they failed to report the act of wrongdoing correctly. Some laws require the witness to report the wrongdoing in writing within a certain period of time after it's discovered. Other laws require the whistleblower to state the specific laws that were broken. The purpose of these requirements is to provide the employer with specificity so it can correct the problem.

[...]

Private-Sector Employees Have It Tough

Most whistleblower laws are intended to protect public-sector employees who report violations affecting public health and safety. Proving public interest is easy for public-sector employees because their work involves public protection. It's not as easy for private-sector employees. Eleven percent of the private-sector whistle-blowers in the sample lost their cases because the matters didn't involve public policy. The case of two nurses working in a private nursing home exemplifies the difficulties private-sector employees can have winning in court even when their cases appear to involve public interest.

Case in point: A hospital fired one of its therapists six days after he told representatives from an accrediting organization during a site visit that the hospital's therapists completed patient charts sometime during their shifts rather than immediately after treating patients as required by the accrediting organization.

The therapist, who had worked for the hospital for 23 years, sued for retaliation and lost because he couldn't convince the courts that charting was a matter of public policy. The therapist argued that the Illinois Medical Patient's Rights Act gives patients the right to sound and consistent care, and failing to immediately chart jeopardizes patient care. The court said it wasn't enough to claim a broad or generalized public policy.

To prevail, the therapist needed to show how a lack of immediate charting violates an Illinois state law, and the therapist wasn't able to find an Illinois law that requires immediate charting. Only the courts can decide whether an issue is a matter of public policy, and this court wasn't willing to find it so.

Five percent of the private-sector employees in this sample lost because they mistakenly filed charges under statutes that covered only public employees. Not all the laws protect private-sector employees. Whistleblowers need to make sure they are covered by the laws they use.

Whistleblowers Try to Protect the Public Interest

Eighty-five percent of the cases involved issues of public health, safety, or interest. Twenty-five percent involved public safety. Fifteen percent involved public health. Sixteen percent involved the misappropriation of public funds. Eighteen percent involved matters of general public interest, and 11 percent involved civil rights violations.

Public employees filed 60 percent of the cases in the sample, and they tended to witness the most serious violations of public policy. Public engineers reported the most serious offenses. These incidents usually involved public exposure to toxic chemicals or waste. Public nurses also reported serious issues. Their complaints usually involved patient neglect and fatal accidents. The complaints of police officers were also very serious and usually involved internal corruption.

Damage awards were often given to whistleblowers who reported serious public policy issues. An analyst in a California public housing authority, for example, reported that someone was leaking confidential bid information. The whistleblower was fired, but was awarded a $1.3 million damage award in court. In Pennsylvania, a housing authority employee reported self-dealing and received a $900,000 damage award for being terminated. These awards were given to whistleblowers reporting irregularities involving public funds.

Large awards were also given to whistleblowers reporting violations of public health and safety. A Connecticut water treatment plant engineer was terminated after reporting plant managers for concealing that the town's water supply was inadequately treated. The court awarded the engineer $127,000 for lost wages. These awards support the assertion that whistleblowers are public employees attempting to resolve serious violations of public policy.

The violations show that 15 percent of the employees accused their employers of issuing false reports. Fourteen percent alleged violations involving air or water quality. Ten percent alleged nepotism or self-dealing. Nine percent alleged patient abuse or neglect. Nine percent alleged discrimination or civil rights violations. Eight percent alleged miscellaneous violations and another eight percent alleged violations of state labor laws or workplace safety.

Laws Used by Whistleblowers

[...]

Most of the employees who sued to appeal decisions that their whistleblowing violated professional codes of conduct lost when the codes required the professionals to maintain client confidentiality. The whistleblowers argued that employers aren't clients, and the codes don't require employee-employer confidentiality. The courts still held these employees to a higher standard of confidentiality. So far, the courts have applied this standard to attorneys, but other professionals with confidentiality clauses in their codes of conduct, such as accountants, could be held to this standard as well.

Most of the whistleblowers in the review lost their lawsuits. 55 percent of the whistleblowers filing under a state whistleblower statute lost their cases. Sixty-four percent filing under a labor law lost, as did 60 percent of those filing under the US Constitution or civil service agreement. Half of the employees appealing a violation of a professional code of conduct lost.

This review couldn't determine why the whistleblowers used the wrong laws or filed in inappropriate courts. It's clear that many of the whistleblowers could have been more successful if they had been smarter about what and where to file. Several factors play a role in deciding under what law and in which court to file.

[...]

Don't Get Caught with Unclean Hands!

Five percent of the whistleblowers failed to receive protection because of their improper conduct. Some of these whistleblowers misused their employers' property; some of them stole it. Employees must ensure their conduct is above scrutiny because some courts will apply the "doctrine of unclean hands" and bar whistleblowers from protection, if they've engaged in misconduct directly related to their complaints.

Case in point: A California quality assurance manager secretly copied confidential patient records to prove that a near-fatal incident was caused by human error after her hospital-employer appeared to be dodging an investigation. The manager pursued an investigation and was fired a few weeks later. The manager sued for wrongful termination and barely prevailed. The lower court applied the doctrine of unclean hands and ruled in favor of the hospital. The manager appealed. The appeals court didn't dismiss the case but significantly limited what the employee could recover because of her unclean hands.

The doctrine of unclean hands can work against employers, just as it does employees. In 2001, a Florida health-care agency submitted documents containing incorrect information to the court. The whistleblower proved the information was false and won her case on those grounds alone. Thus, it's important for employers and employees to comport themselves with integrity.

Whistleblowers who commit unlawful acts to advance their cases don't do well in court, but neither do whistleblowers who refuse to commit unlawful acts on behalf of their employers. Most state whistleblower laws are designed to protect employees that refuse to commit unlawful acts, but it can be difficult to receive that protection.

Case in point: A Texas deckhand was asked to pump the bilges of the boat into the water, despite a placard on the boat, which stated that pumping bilges into the water was illegal. The deckhand confirmed with the US Coast Guard that the practice was illegal. The deckhand refused to pump the bilges and was fired. He sued for wrongful discharge and prevailed because the court upheld the public policy doctrine that prevents the termination of at-will employees for refusing to perform illegal acts.

The deckhand above prevailed, but many others haven't been as fortunate. A Florida tugboat captain, for example, was fired after he refused to make an 18-hour trip in contravention to the federal safety regulations. The captain lost in court, even though the Florida whistleblower law states that employers can't retaliate against employees for refusing to participate in unlawful activities. Employees such as the tugboat captain might manage to avoid breaking the law, but they may have to sacrifice their jobs to do so.

Implications

The review of this sample of cases helps provide some important insights into actual whistleblowing incidents. The review shows that even when well-intentioned employees feel they're doing the right thing by reporting acts of wrongdoing, their reports aren't always well received. The findings also suggest that employees who witness acts of wrongdoing should seek legal counsel before acting.

The cases didn't involve any whistleblowers who also happened to be CFEs, but CFEs might run into the same types of problems. CFEs should learn when, where, and how to report fraudulent acts before they blow the whistle, so they can comply with the procedures required to receive protection.

This review looked at only a sample of the state-level cases filed against employers for retaliation. But it does highlight the fact that whistleblower cases can be difficult to prove, and it's best that all involved (including CFEs) should be knowledgeable about the laws involved and seek legal guidance early.

Blowing the Whistle May Significantly Affect One's Personal Life

Brian Martin

Dr. Brian Martin is a professor at the University of Wollongong in Australia. His research covers topics such as power within the field of science, information in free societies, and similar areas.

Whistleblowing means speaking out in the public interest, and in bioweapons research there are many potential reasons for doing this. Perhaps a rogue researcher is pursuing dangerous experiments, or defensive research is being subtly oriented in offensive directions. Perhaps someone is releasing sensitive information without authorization; safety systems are being neglected; data are being forged; or the lab is pursuing research, under government instructions, that the government is denying publicly.

But is it wise to speak out? What are the risks? Consider these examples.

On 22 July 2005, Charles de Menezes, having just entered a train, was shot in the head seven times by London police. The police claimed he was wearing a bulky coat and had jumped over the ticket barrier and had run to the train. But Lana Vandenberghe knew the police were lying. She worked for the Independent Police Complaints Commission and had access to evidence presented at the commission's inquiry into the shooting. She leaked information to a television journalist—and then was subject to reprisals by the police. In a dawn raid on 21 September 2005, ten police officers broke down her door and arrested her. She was kept in a cell without access to a lawyer for eight hours and threatened by police that she could go to prison. She said: 'It never crossed my mind that I would be treated as if I was a criminal for telling the truth. Unlike the police, I hadn't killed an innocent person' (Sanderson, 2006).

"Whistleblowers: risks and skills," by Brian Martin. Reprinted by permission.

Teresa Chambers was chief of the US Park Police, like a municipal police department but with responsibility for national parks and monuments, mainly in the Washington, DC, area. It had over 600 officers. In the aftermath of 9/11 the Park Police were given additional anti-terrorism responsibilities, but no additional funding. Chambers spoke regularly to the media; it was part of her job. In December 2003, she spoke to a *Washington Post* journalist, saying anti-terrorism duties meant less services in regular park functions and asking for a greater budget to cover all of the service's tasks. Soon after, she was stripped of her gun and badge—a tremendous humiliation—and put on leave, and was later terminated.

Thomas Bittler and Ray Guagliardi worked for the US Transportation Security Administration (TSA). In 2003, while serving as training coordinators at Buffalo Niagara International Airport, they noticed numerous violations of regulations for inspecting baggage, for example, inadequate inspections following alarms. They reported their concerns to their boss, which led nowhere, so they wrote to TSA headquarters. The result: they lost their jobs two months later, officially due to a staff restructure. However, both men say TSA officials told them that they should never have complained. According to Bittler, one supervisor said: "If you people would just learn to shut your mouths, you would still have your jobs."

Richard Levernier was a nuclear security professional with 23 years' experience. After 9/11, he raised concerns with the Department of Energy about the vulnerability of US nuclear power plants to terrorist attack, for example pointing out that contingency plans assumed terrorists would both enter and exit facilities, therefore not addressing the risk of suicide attacks. His security clearance was withdrawn and he was relegated to a basement office coordinating departmental travel, his career in nuclear security terminated. Levernier went to the Office of Special Counsel (OSC), the body responsible for US federal whistleblower matters. Four years later, the OSC vindicated Levernier and ruled that the Department of Energy's retaliation was illegal—but the OSC had no power to restore Levernier's security clearance, which remained revoked.

Whistleblowing definitely is a risky business. These examples are just a sample of thousands of similar cases, although each one is far more complicated than can be conveyed by a short summary.

The typical whistleblower is a conscientious employee who believes the system works. When such an employee sees something wrong, their natural response is to report it. This is often a serious mistake.

Some of the common methods used against whistleblowers are ostracism, harassment, spreading of rumours, reprimands, punitive transfers, threats, referral to psychiatrists, demotion, dismissal and blacklisting. To simply list these methods gives only a faint indication of the tremendous damage they do. Ostracism is a common experience: bosses shun the whistleblower and so do most other workers out of fear for their own jobs. Because validation by peers and supervisors is vital for a worker's self-esteem, ostracism is extremely hard to handle. Yet this is just one of many reprisals commonly suffered by whistleblowers.

[...]

Skills

[...]

A person known for telling lies, getting drunk, shouting abuse or undermining colleagues will have much less credibility than one known for honesty, sobriety, politeness and generosity.

There are ways around a bad reputation. One of the best is anonymity. Instead of speaking out, leak documents to those who will act on them. The documents will need to be good enough to stand on their own, without personal recommendation and interpretation. Leaking has the great advantage of lowering the risk of reprisals. Nevertheless, it is not easy to be an effective 'leaker' because employers have so many ways of tracking them down. Some photocopiers leave distinctive marks: taking photocopies of photocopies is a wise precaution. Even without a direct physical link, the leaker can sometimes be identified by the documents revealed. A nasty employer will retaliate by dismissing one or more people, even if they are not responsible, making the leaker feel guilty for causing damage to the careers of co-workers.

An intermediate option is to be a leaker and be known to a few individuals who are in receipt of the leaked documents. In this case, personal credibility is again important, as is secrecy when communicating with contacts. The other option is to go public. This can lead to dismissal or denial of privileges, which reduces or terminates access to documents. As a result, it is vital to collect all possible documents first.

Once whistleblowers are identified, it is almost certain that efforts will be made to tarnish their reputation. Any blemish will be uncovered and publicized. School principals have been known to go through personal files of whistleblowing teachers and unearth and make known pupil complaints against the teacher dating five or ten years earlier. Having a totally unblemished record is not full protection because damaging documents may be manufactured and fictitious stories created to discredit the whistleblower. But such attempts are less likely to be successful if the person has a good reputation and good relationships.

[...]

The next question is who to approach. This is where good judgement is at a premium. For something trivial, it is best to use the usual channels—it looks silly to go straight to the auditors about a missing £10. But something seemingly trivial is occasionally linked to something bigger: the missing £10 might be part of a long-running scam.

The general rule is that it is unwise to trust anyone who has a vested interest in hiding the truth. This means that the safest people to approach are the ones right outside the organization. But rather than rule anyone out automatically, it is worth considering all possible allies.

Co-workers are an obvious possibility. Half a dozen workers making a claim are far more powerful and convincing than a single one; finding even a single other person as an ally is far better than going it alone. Who to approach? This is the tricky part. Approaching the wrong person could be disastrous: the boss is quietly informed and suddenly all your access to materials is denied, your co-workers stay away and your security clearance is withdrawn. On the other hand, finding the right person can make an enormous difference, with access to additional information, contacts and wise advice.

In such situations, caution is advisable. If there are one or two people you trust implicitly, you can confide in them and share ideas about who else to approach. But if you do not have a good sense of who is trustworthy, it may be worth seeking advice. Often there are some experienced members of the organization who have a good sense of people and organizational dynamics. Getting to know these experienced members is worthwhile. You can start by asking some innocent questions, such as how to help a colleague who is having difficulties with an experiment or a dispute over co-authorship—some sort of dilemma that is different from, but with structural similarities to, the one that concerns you. In this way, you can learn about who is trustworthy, who is self-seeking and who should be avoided.

If one or more co-workers can be brought into a circle of concern, this is a great beginning. If not, you will have to operate alone in the organization. The next step is whether to approach anyone else.

[...]

Conclusions

The best people to expose problems within organizations are those who see them up close: the workers. But people who speak out often suffer reprisals. The normal solution to this problem is whistleblower protection: laws and procedures to protect those who make public interest disclosures. Unfortunately, the track record of whistleblower protection measures—whistleblower laws, hotlines, ombudsmen and the like—is abysmal. In many cases, these formal processes give only an illusion of protection. Codes of ethics seem similarly impotent in the face of the problems.

An alternative to whistleblower protection is fostering effective organizational action. This requires a shift in mindset. Rather than thinking: 'I observed a problem, so I'll speak out about it', the alternative is: 'I observed a problem, so I'll figure out the best way to be effective in dealing with it.' If there is a single rule for people wanting to address an organizational problem, it is to seek advice before acting, including advice from people who know a lot about how organizations operate and how to tackle social problems. Part of the likely advice is that just speaking out, without preparation, is unwise—in fact, it's likely to be disastrous. A lot of preparation is needed, including gathering information, recruiting allies, developing skills and planning a course of action.

Scientists are familiar with the discrepancy between everyday perceptions of the world and scientific understandings. The world may appear flat, the sun may appear to move across the sky and desks may appear to be solid; scientists, using their skills and tools, have arrived at more sophisticated and powerful understandings, some of which have become common knowledge.

Yet, when it comes to the social world, most scientists, like most other workers, are naïve observers, treating social life in terms of surface understandings, including that a report about a problem will be investigated, that whistleblower laws protect whistleblowers and that courts and official agencies dispense justice. Research and the accumulated experience of whistleblower advisers point to different realities: workers who report a problem may be targeted with reprisals; whistleblower laws do not provide protection; and official channels do not dispense justice.

Whistleblowers often suffer a related misconception: their own case is different. Even when they hear about the treatment of other whistleblowers, they think their experience will be different because they know they are right: they have truth on their side. Sadly, this is no protection. The key to progress in science, and in whistleblowing, is learning from the experience of others and developing the skills, acquiring the resources and building the networks to do better.

Extensive Whistleblower Protections Are in Place in Many Countries

Norm Keith, Shane Todd, and Carla Oliver

Norm Keith is a lawyer whose interests center on labor, employment, regulatory, and government investigations. Shane Todd is an author with White Collar Post, *which publicizes instances of white-collar crime, and Carla Oliver is a Toronto-based occupational health and safety and human resources consultant. All three work with the Fasken firm in Toronto.*

The international landscape of whistleblowing is changing dramatically and quickly. The Supreme Court of Canada was the first national high court in the world to recognize and protect the role of whistleblowers, their identity, and immunity from disclosure and criminal prosecution. In its decision involving the World Bank Group, the Court addressed the subject of whistleblower immunity in an international case. The opening paragraph of the Supreme Court judgment, delivered by Justices Moldaver and Côté, reads as:

> Corruption is a significant obstacle to international development. It undermines confidence in public institutions, diverts funds from those who are in great need of financial support, and violates business integrity. Corruption often transcends borders. In order to tackle this global problem, worldwide cooperation is needed. When international financial organizations, such as the appellant World Bank Group, share information gathered from informants across the world with the law enforcement agencies of member states, they help achieve what neither could

do on their own. (*World Bank Grp. v. Wallace*, 2016 SCC 15, para. 1 (Can.).)

[…]

United States

[…]

On July 21, 2010, President Obama signed into law the Dodd-Frank Wall Street Reform and Consumer Protection Act (Dodd-Frank Act). (Pub. L. No. 111-203, § 922(a), 124 Stat. 1376, 1841 (2010).) The Dodd-Frank Act initiated a massive overhaul of the US financial sector and introduced a range of new and improved whistleblower protection laws.

Importantly, the Dodd-Frank Act amended the 1934 Securities and Exchange Act by adding section 21F, entitled "Securities Whistleblower Incentives and Protection." (US SEC. & EXCH. COMM'N, 2015 ANNUAL REPORT TO CONGRESS ON THE DODD-FRANK WHISTLEBLOWER PROGRAM 4 (2015) [hereinafter SEC REPORT], *available at* http://tinyurl.com/p3k5gdj.) Section 21F allows the SEC to make monetary awards to individuals who voluntarily provide original information that leads to successful enforcement actions resulting in monetary sanctions over $1 million. To administer the whistleblower program, the Dodd-Frank Act established the Office of the Whistleblower (OWB)—a separate office of the SEC's Division of Enforcement. (*Id.*) Section 924(d) of the Dodd-Frank Act requires the OWB to report to Congress about its activities on an annual basis. (*Id.*)

Whistleblower awards can be up to 30 percent of the recovered proceeds in America. The SEC may increase or decrease a financial award depending on the circumstances. Awards may be increased depending on the nature and significance of the information to the enforcement activity, the assistance provided by the whistleblower, whether and the extent to which the individual participated in internal compliance systems, and whether the making of an award in the circumstances would further law enforcement's interest in an effective whistleblowing program. (17 C.F.R. § 240.21F-6.) The SEC may decrease a financial award if the whistleblower was culpable or involved in the securities violation. In considering whether to decrease an award, the SEC considers the whistleblower's role, education, training, experience and responsibility, knowledge of wrongdoing, financial benefit, prior record (if any), egregiousness of conduct, and whether he or she knowingly interfered with an SEC investigation. (*Id.*)

Since 2011, the SEC has paid out more than $67 million to 29 whistleblowers, and by the end of fiscal year 2015 had received 14,116 tips. (SEC REPORT, *supra*, at 21; Press Release 2016-91, SEC, SEC Awards More Than $5 Million to Whistleblower (May 17, 2016), http://tinyurl.com/h9dqq62.) The largest SEC awards to date are $30 million and $14 million. (Press Release 2014-206, SEC, SEC Announces Largest-Ever Whistleblower Award (Sept. 22, 2014), http://tinyurl.com/zw6f66o; Press Release 2013-209, SEC, SEC Awards More Than $14 Million to Whistleblower (Oct. 1, 2013), http://tinyurl.com/zajbwnq.) Two recent large awards include a $3.5 million award on May 13, 2016, to a whistleblower who provided information during an ongoing investigation that strengthened the SEC's case, and a $5 million award on May 17, 2016, to a former company insider whose detailed tip led the SEC to uncover securities violations. (Whistleblower Award Proceeding, Exchange Act Release No. 77833 (May 13, 2016); Press Release 2016-91, *supra*.)

In addition to creating a monetary incentive program, the Dodd-Frank Act explicitly prohibits reprisal against whistleblowers who report corporate wrongdoing, particularly in regard to securities violations. The Dodd-Frank Act also expanded the antiretaliation provisions of SOX to apply to employees of subsidiaries of publicly traded companies, in addition to employees of publicly traded companies. The Dodd-Frank Act also doubled the statutory filing period for SOX retaliation complaints from 90 to 180 days and gave parties the right to a jury trial in district court actions. Finally, the Dodd-Frank Act created a new cause of action allowing whistleblowers to sue in federal court if their employers retaliated against them for disclosing information about their employer to the SEC.

Canada

There is less comprehensive whistleblowing legislation in Canada compared to the United States.

[...]

Section 19 of the PSDPA provides that "[n]o person shall take any reprisal against a public servant or direct that one be taken against a public servant." Sections 19.1(1) and (2) provide that where a public servant or former public servant believes, on reasonable grounds, that a reprisal has been taken against him or her, the public servant may file a complaint within 60 days with the Office of the Public Sector Integrity Commissioner, a new agency created under the PSDPA. The commissioner reviews all complaints and may investigate if there are grounds to believe a reprisal has been taken. After investigating, the commissioner may refer a reprisal complaint to the Public Servants Disclosure Protection Tribunal, a quasi-judicial body that adjudicates reprisal complaints. The tribunal has the power to order remedies for the complainant and to make orders against a person who has engaged in a reprisal. In addition to any other applicable legal penalty, a public servant who has engaged in a reprisal may be subject to disciplinary action up to termination of employment as determined by the tribunal. (*Id.* at sec. 9.)

The PSDPA, the commissioner, and the tribunal have been the subject of criticism. Critics note that perpetrators can escape punishment under the PSDPA regime by pursuing employment in the private sector. Compounding this issue is the fact that the commissioner does not disclose the identities of wrongdoers, which means that prospective employers do not become aware of prior misconduct. (TI-CAN REPORT, *supra*, at 10.) In addition, over a seven-year period, only six out of 140 reprisal cases were referred by the commissioner to the tribunal. Of these six cases, the commissioner declined to ask the tribunal for disciplinary actions against the employers despite identifying specific acts of reprisal. As well, during Christiane Ouimet's three-year tenure as commissioner from 2007 to 2010, no wrongdoing or reprisals were found among the more than 200 complaints filed. (*Id.* at 11.)

[…]

Europe

Over the past 20 years, whistleblower protection legislation has been slowly gaining momentum within the European Union (EU). (*See* MARK WORTH, TRANSPARENCY INT'L, WHISTLEBLOWING IN EUROPE: LEGAL PROTECTIONS FOR WHISTLEBLOWERS IN THE EU (2013) [hereinafter TI-EU REPORT], http://tinyurl.com/zpvgct8.)

[…]

United Kingdom

The United Kingdom enacted the EU's first comprehensive whistleblower legislation in 1998, the Public Interest Disclosure Act (PIDA). PIDA covers nearly all employees in the public, private, and nonprofit sectors, as well as contractors, trainees, and U.K. workers based overseas. (*Id.* at 10.)

PIDA gives workers and employees the right to bring a claim in the employment tribunal for compensation if they suffer reprisal. (PUB. CONCERN AT WORK, IS THE LAW PROTECTING WHISTLEBLOWERS? A REVIEW OF PIDA CLAIMS 6 (2015) [hereinafter PCAW REPORT], available at http://tinyurl.com/za3sbne.) PIDA also provides an "after the event" remedy for victimized whistleblowers rather than only preventing such victimization from taking place. PIDA protection applies from the outset of employment, which means there is no requirement that the employee work for a qualifying period, as with ordinary unfair dismissal claims. PIDA is based on a "tiered" system of disclosure where whistleblowers can disclose information to their employer, regulatory agencies, external individuals such as members of Parliament, or directly to the media. Accuracy standards increase with each tier, meaning whistleblower reports must be more accurate if they are reported externally in order for the whistleblower to be legally protected. (TI-EU REPORT, supra, at 83.)

Under PIDA, employers must prove that any action taken against an employee or worker was not motivated by the fact that an employee was a whistleblower. In addition to financial losses, employees can also claim compensation for aggravated damages and injury to their feelings. One such award reached £5 million. (*Id.*)

[…]

Conclusion

The enactment and enforcement of whistleblowing legislation has in recent years become a central element in the fight against corruption. To this end, countries around the world, but particularly in Asia, Europe, and North America, have enacted whistleblower protections aimed at providing safe and reliable avenues for corporate and government employees to report misconduct. While much has been achieved in this regard, many countries still have little or no whistleblower protections. In addition, despite calls for international cooperation and legal frameworks, whistleblower legislation remains predominantly a national or regional issue.

Regardless of the presence or absence of whistleblower protections in a particular jurisdiction, public and private organizations can through careful advance planning establish an organizational whistleblowing system. Subject to applicable law, the best practices outlined above can assist in establishing a clear and effective internal whistleblowing system. These best practices focus on six broad areas: (1) scope, clarity, and communication of internal reporting procedures; (2) protecting whistleblower identity and the contents of reports; (3) creating a culture that facilitates internal compliance; (4) establishing and enforcing antireprisal protections; (5) screening, investigating, and acting on credible reports; and (6) auditing the system to ensure its proper implementation and operation. By implementing these best practices and complying with applicable local law, the resulting system should encourage early and internal reporting of wrongdoing, and allow organizations to implement strategies to control legal and reputational risks.

Regardless of Identity, Those Who Leak Information Face Similar Consequences

Sharon D. Nelson and John W. Simek

Sharon D. Nelson is the president of Sensei Enterprises, a digital forensics and information technology firm. John W. Simek is the vice president of Sensei Enterprises. They have collaborated on several books.

Perfectly normal people grow slightly lunatic when talking about Edward Snowden. Cries of treason were loud at the beginning. As time and revelations of National Security Agency (NSA) surveillance went on, more and more people used the word "whistleblower" rather than "traitor." In December the NSA itself talked about amnesty for Snowden—nixed by the federal government, at least for now. He cannot do what so many want—give the documents back. Clearly, they are in the hands of journalists across the globe. Recent revelations have shaken lawyers, especially at large and global firms, and it's clear we too will have to live in what one journalist called the "post-Snowden era." So let's get to know him.

Who Is Edward Snowden?

Snowden was born on June 21, 1983. Friends and neighbors described him as shy, quiet and nice. His father called him a deep thinker. He was fascinated by Japanese culture and, as a young adult, listed Buddhism as his religion on a military recruitment form. He once told the *Washington Post* that he was an ascetic, rarely left home and had few needs.

Without going into too much detail, he joined the CIA in 2006 as a systems administrator and telecommunications systems officer. In 2007 the CIA stationed him with diplomatic cover in Geneva, where he was responsible for network security.

He resigned from the CIA in February 2009 and went to work for Dell and was stationed in an NSA facility in Japan, where he worked as a contractor. In April 2012 he relocated to Hawaii, and continued to work for Dell until early 2013, when he took a new job with Booz Allen Hamilton. It was at an NSA facility in Hawaii that Snowden first began downloading evidence of the US government's electronic spying program while still employed by Dell. However, at Booz Allen he was one of approximately 1,000 NSA system administrators allowed to look at many parts of the network without leaving an electronic trail and succeeded in getting flash drives into a secure environment.

Snowden has said he took a pay cut to work with Booz Allen so he could gather data about global NSA surveillance and leak it. According to Booz Allen, Snowden's employment was terminated on June 10, 2013, "for violations of the firm's code of ethics and firm policy."

A former NSA co-worker told *Forbes* that although the NSA was full of smart people, Snowden was "a genius among geniuses." He was described as a "principled and ultra-competent, if somewhat eccentric employee, and one who earned the access used to pull off his leak by impressing superiors with sheer talent." Snowden created a backup system for the NSA that was implemented, and he often pointed out security bugs to the agency. The former colleague said Snowden was "given full administrator privileges, with virtually unlimited access to NSA data" because he could "do things nobody else could." Snowden had been offered a position on the NSA's elite staff of hackers, Tailored Access Operations, but turned it down for the contractor position at Booz Allen.

Snowden kept a copy of the US Constitution on his desk to cite when arguing against NSA activities he thought might violate it, *Forbes* reported. He has said many times that he tried to get people in the NSA to recognize that many of its activities were illegal—and that many were indeed deeply concerned—but no one wanted to mount a charge against the agency.

Though several government officials have tried to say that his actions were directed by a foreign power, there is simply no evidence of that, according to the *New York Times*. His former colleague, while disagreeing with his methods, told *Forbes*, "I understand why he did it. I won't call him a hero, but he's sure as hell no traitor."

What Has He Revealed Thus Far?

On May 20, 2013, Snowden flew to Hong Kong. He was there when the initial articles based on the leaked documents were published, beginning on June 5. A continuing series of articles were distributed worldwide by, most notably, the *Guardian* (Britain), *Der Spiegel* (Germany), the *Washington Post* and the *New York Times*. Here's what we now know:

- The first program to be revealed was PRISM, which allows for court-approved, front-door access to Americans' Google and Yahoo accounts.
- A report also revealed details of Tempora, a British black operations surveillance program run by the NSA's British partner, GCHQ. The initial reports included details about an NSA call database, Boundless Informant; a secret court order requiring Verizon to hand the NSA millions of Americans' phone records daily; the surveillance of French citizens' phone and Internet records; and surveillance of "high-profile individuals from the world of business or politics," according the *The Local*, a French news publication in English.
- Next was XKeyscore, which allows for the collection of "nearly everything a typical user does on the Internet," which was described by the *Guardian* as a program that "shed light" on one of Snowden's more contentious claims: "I, sitting at my desk [could] wiretap anyone, from you or

your accountant, to a federal judge or even the president, if I had a personal email."

- It was revealed that the NSA was harvesting millions of emails and instant messaging contact lists, searching email content, tracking and mapping the location of cellphones, undermining encryption via Bullrun, and that the agency was using cookies to "piggyback" on the same tools used by Internet advertisers "to pinpoint targets for government hacking and to bolster surveillance." The NSA was shown to be "secretly" tapping into Yahoo and Google data centers to collect information from "hundreds of millions" of account holders worldwide by tapping undersea cables using the MUSCULAR program.

- Leaked documents showed that NSA agents spied on their "love interests," a practice NSA employees termed "LOVEINT." The NSA was also shown to be tracking the online sexual activity of people they termed "radicalizers" in order to discredit them.

- Snowden's disclosures created tension between the US and some of its close allies, revealing that the US had spied on Brazil, France, Mexico, Britain, China, Germany and Spain as well as 35 world leaders, most notably German Chancellor Angela Merkel, who said "spying among friends" was "unacceptable" and compared the NSA with the Stasi.

- The NSA's top-secret "black budget" exposed the "successes and failures" of the 16 spy agencies comprising the US intelligence community and revealed that the NSA was paying private American tech companies for "clandestine access" to their communications networks. The agencies were allotted $52 billion for the 2013 fiscal year.

- An NSA mission statement titled "Sigint Strategy 2012–2016" affirmed that the NSA plans to continue expansion of surveillance activities. Its stated goal was to "dramatically increase mastery of the global network" and "acquire the

capabilities to gather intelligence on anyone, anytime, anywhere."
- The infamous NSA ANT catalog was revealed, which offers a remarkable number of products available to the NSA and others to perform surveillance activities.
- The NSA spies on WikiLeaks and records information about its visitors.
- Apparently, most recently, the NSA has received attorney-client communications from its counterpart in Australia.

How Did He Gather All the Data?

Snowden gathered information in a couple of ways. He used easily available Web crawler software to scrape data out of the NSA's systems while he did his day job. Yes, much of it was automated. So this was a low-tech, nearly amateur attack from the inside, and it is remarkable that there were not systems in place to detect it.

How many files did he access? Intelligence officials told the US House of Representatives that he accessed 1.7 million files. These files include shared "wikis" to which intelligence analysts, operatives and others contributed their knowledge.

Embarrassed NSA officials say that Snowden's activities would have been picked up if he had worked at the NSA headquarters in Fort Meade, Maryland, which was equipped with software designed to detect large volumes of data being accessed. But the Hawaii facility had not yet been upgraded with modern security measures.

He was challenged a couple of times, but his explanations sounded rational in light of his duties backing up computer systems and moving information systems.

What Snowden really discovered was that while the NSA has huge electronic barriers to keep out foreign intruders, the protections it had against insiders were rudimentary. Officials have said that no one was looking "inside" the system in Hawaii for strange activity. Remarkable. And, apparently, it remains true that the NSA doesn't actually know what data Snowden possesses, a testament to some of the lousiest security we've seen anywhere.

What Does All This Mean for Law Firms?

The *New York Times* broke an amazing story on Feb. 15. A top-secret document, dated February 2013, demonstrated that an American law firm was monitored while representing a foreign government in trade disputes with the US. The government of Indonesia had retained the law firm for help in trade talks. The document reports that the NSA's Australian counterpart, the Australian Signals Directorate, notified the NSA that it was conducting surveillance of the talks, including communications between Indonesian officials and the American law firm, and it offered to share the information.

The Australians told officials at an NSA liaison office in Canberra, Australia, that "information covered by attorney-client privilege may be included" in the intelligence gathering, according to the document, a monthly bulletin from the Canberra office. The law firm was not identified, but Mayer Brown, a Chicago-based global firm, was then advising the Indonesian government on several trade issues.

On behalf of the Australians, the liaison officials asked the NSA General Counsel's Office for guidance about the spying. The bulletin notes only that the counsel's office "provided clear guidance" and that the Australian agency "has been able to continue to cover the talks, providing highly useful intelligence for interested US customers."

The NSA declined to answer questions about the reported surveillance, including whether information involving the American law firm was shared with US trade officials or negotiators, the *Times* reported.

Note that this is not a story of tracking down terrorists. This is business espionage, pure and simple—something that Snowden has pointed out frequently.

In a statement to the *New York Times*, the NSA declined to comment on the details included in the Snowden document. Broadly speaking, the agency said, "Any allegation that the NSA relies on foreign partners to circumvent US law is absolutely false. The National Security Agency does not ask its foreign partners to undertake any intelligence activity that the US government would be legally prohibited from undertaking itself."

Unfortunately, the NSA's credibility is zilch. Our prediction is that law firms, in sensitive matters, may take an Old World approach and dispatch lawyers to talk to clients in person, and not necessarily in a setting where surveillance might be expected. Remember the old movie scenes of international spies talking to their informers in parks? What's old may well be new again.

Following news reports that a foreign ally of a US intelligence agency may have spied on a Big Law firm, the ABA asked the director of the NSA and its general counsel for an explanation of how it handles attorney-client privilege. In a letter written on February 20, ABA President James R. Silkenat asked the NSA's director for an explanation of what policies and practices the NSA has in place to protect confidential information protected by the attorney-client privilege that may be received or intercepted—and whether those policies and practices were complied with in the alleged law firm incident. On March 10, NSA Director Gen. Keith Alexander responded with a letter assuring that the NSA is "firmly committed to the rule of law and the bedrock legal principle of attorney-client privilege." While the letter's tone is reassuring, it doesn't hold up on close examination. Weasel words abound. One notable example: The letter says the NSA does not "ask" foreign partners to conduct activity prohibited under US law. The truth is that it doesn't have to ask. The voluntary sharing of information between the Five Eyes alliance (US, UK, New Zealand, Australia and Canada) has already been well established. One of several stories involves our good buddies in Britain tapping cables and cheerfully turning over vast amounts of the personal information of US citizens to the NSA.

For more than a year, we have told audiences that it was our assumption that the NSA (and perhaps others) were spying on US law firms. Think about it. The US government, mostly the FBI and the Secret Service, has been coming to law firms and advising them that they had been breached by foreign governments, hackers, etc. Audiences keep asking, "How did they know?" We thought the only logical answer much of the time was that the NSA or one of its international counterparts in the Five Eyes alliance had already infiltrated the law firms and watched the other intruders come through the door. Since we now know that they are intercepting law firm communications, why would they hesitate to penetrate law firm networks?

Why Did Snowden Do It?

In a December 2013 letter to the people of Brazil, Snowden wrote, "There is a huge difference between legal programs, legitimate spying…and these programs of dragnet mass surveillance that put entire populations under an all-seeing eye and save copies forever…These programs were never about terrorism: They're about economic spying, social control and diplomatic manipulation. They're about power."

Snowden's identity was made public by the *Guardian* at his request on June 9, 2013. He explained, "I have no intention of hiding who I am because I know I have done nothing wrong." He added that by revealing his identity he hoped to protect his colleagues from being subjected to a hunt to determine who had been responsible for the leaks. Snowden explained his actions, saying, "I didn't want to change society. I wanted to give society a chance to determine if it should change itself. All I wanted was for the public to be able to have a say in how they are governed."

When Snowden met with representatives of human rights organizations, he said: The 4th and 5th Amendments to the Constitution of my country, Article 12 of the Universal Declaration of Human Rights, and numerous statutes and treaties forbid such systems of massive, pervasive surveillance. While the US

Constitution marks these programs as illegal, my government argues that secret court rulings, which the world is not permitted to see, somehow legitimize an illegal affair…I believe in the principle declared at Nuremberg in 1945: Individuals have international duties which transcend the national obligations of obedience. Therefore individual citizens have the duty to violate domestic laws to prevent crimes against peace and humanity from occurring.

Snowden said that the system for reporting problems does not work. "You have to report wrongdoing to those most responsible for it." He pointed out the lack of whistleblower protection for government contractors, the use of the 1917 Espionage Act to prosecute leakers and his belief that had he used internal mechanisms to "sound the alarm," his revelations "would have been buried forever." That sounds about right to us.

Snowden's Future—And What It Means to Us

Simply put, Snowden's future is bleak. He lives in a secret location in Russia, where Putin is no doubt happy to have him be a continuing irritant to the US. Russia was certainly not on Snowden's list of places to land, but he had little choice once his passport was revoked while in the Moscow airport. His temporary asylum can be renewed annually and probably will be.

Clearly, he believes it was worth it. He has made a difference insofar as there is intense scrutiny by many, including law firms, of potential "watchers," foreign and domestic. And we think a man who keeps a copy of the Constitution on his desk to refute superiors would do it again—in a heartbeat.

As for lawyers, there are high-level talks going on at many major law firms and a lot of chatter on the wire about the need to keep sensitive data out of email, telephone conversations and videoconferencing systems. Perhaps lawyers will actually use encryption to protect their client's confidential data and communications instead of constantly complaining that it is too difficult.

We think there is a strong likelihood that distrust of state-sponsored surveillance will have us harking back to the old days of face-to-face communication in places unlikely to have camera or audio surveillance. Graffiti seen recently in a restroom stall at a McDonald's resonated with author Nelson: It said simply, "Orwell was Right." And so he was.

Chapter 3

Should Whistleblowers Be Financially Compensated?

Case Studies Reveal the Complexity of Whistleblower Compensation

Lachlan Colquhoun

Over the last four decades, Lachlan Colquhoun has worked as a journalist for the Financial Times, *the* London Evening Standard, *and other papers. His interests include technology, government, and the corporate world.*

As many corporate whistleblowers discover, doing the right thing isn't always rewarded. Instead, telling the truth can be followed by retribution and career ruin. Ahead of their appearance at the World Congress of Accountants (WCOA), Wendy Addison, Sylvain Mansotte and Michael Woodford ask: How do we make it safe to speak up?

For most people who become whistleblowers, it is a life-changing experience. In the case of Wendy Addison, who will be sharing her story at the World Congress of Accountants (WCOA), this meant going from her dream job as CFO of a listed company in her native South Africa to homeless and begging on the streets of London.

"I was unemployed for 11 years and I was psychologically broken," she says. "My only focus was on survival."

From this low point, Addison embarked on a path of research in social science and neuroscience, ultimately forming a consultancy called SpeakOut SpeakUp, which not only addresses whistleblowing, but seeks to change organisational behaviour so that whistleblowing is no longer necessary.

"Now, my life is woven with such richness, in terms of the people I meet all over the world," Addison says. "When I contrast that with the corporate ambitions I had when I was in my 30s, I can only celebrate where I have got to."

Michael Woodford's three-decade career in the UK for Japanese camera manufacturer Olympus culminated in his appointment as the company's first non-Japanese chief executive in 2011. Only months later, he was dismissed in a dramatic boardroom showdown after blowing the whistle on a £1 billion fraud linked to the Japanese yakuza (organised crime syndicate).

It was Woodford's last corporate role; now he devotes his time to philanthropy and a road safety charity in Asia.

"I thought I was going to be assassinated," Woodford says. "It completely changed my world and I have no stomach for corporate life now. I am a lone wolf who has been thrown out of the pack and I don't want to go back."

Woodford also "bangs the drum" for better corporate behaviour and consults to major corporates around the world, in addition to a role as patron with European whistleblowing charity Public Concern at Work.

How Much Has Changed?

Despite legislative progress in the UK through the *Public Interest Disclosure Act 1998*, Woodford is still cynical about the corporate world's embrace of whistleblowing.

"If you are a high-paid director of a listed company, it is in your self-interest as much as anything to do the right thing," he says. "You want your systems to be robust, so your company doesn't commit acts where you can be held responsible for malfeasance. Who wants that?"

Closer to home, Sylvain Mansotte discovered a long-running fraud in the procurement area of construction giant Leighton Holdings only weeks after he joined in 2013.

Mansotte uncovered a A$20 million fake invoicing fraud, and his whistleblowing resulted in a 15-year jail sentence for former finance manager Damian O'Carrigan, who had used the proceeds to fund an extravagant lifestyle of overseas holidays, racehorses and mistresses.

"My entire world turned upside down," Mansotte says. "I was the guy with the gun in his hand, and I knew if I pulled that trigger I could destroy the life of a family and a guy who had been at Leighton for 30 years and was six months from retirement."

Although he was promoted at Leighton, Mansotte left in 2015 to develop an online solution that has developed into Whispli, a secure and anonymous two-way communication solution used not just for corporate whistleblowing, but for reporting sexual harassment and bullying in schools and universities.

It is a product that came directly from Mansotte's own whistleblowing experience. He was initially reluctant to approach any of his colleagues, and did not feel confident speaking to the third-party organisation appointed by the company because it would compromise the anonymity he felt necessary.

His French accent, he believed, was a giveaway and would have the unwelcome consequence of identifying him. "I was blaming myself for uncovering something," Mansotte says. "Do you go to a third party who knows nothing about you, and who is potentially going to go back to your organisation and tell them?

My fear was that the company would come back to me and say, 'You went to that third party and that was wrong for you to talk about. Wrong! Here's the door, see you later.'"

A Safer Way to Blow the Whistle

Users of Whispli can communicate anonymously and continuously with either designated areas in the organisation or with third parties. After initial contact, they can answer questions and provide more details and progress the issue, accessing Whispli from anywhere using a password and a case identification number.

"It creates one single source for the reporting of misconduct and wrongdoing," Mansotte says. "Some clients have said they get four times as many reports using Whispli, so it's definitely helping people come forward."

After its adoption by hundreds of organisations around the world, such as Coca-Cola, Qantas, and Oxfam, Mansotte is leaving Australia for Boston [in the US] this year to continue to drive his business; one that he would never have had but for his whistleblowing experience.

"It's been a massive turnaround in my life but it's been a good one," Mansotte says. "I'm one of the lucky ones."

Supporting Whistleblowers

Those three whistleblowing cases all go back years, and in the duration there have been significant legislative and cultural shifts. In Australia and New Zealand, the first wide-ranging national research into whistleblowing—called "Whistling While They Work"—drew responses from 702 public, private sector and not-for-profit organisations.

The study, completed by Griffith University, Australian National University, University of Sydney and supported by 22 regulatory and professional organisations, including CPA Australia, found that while 90 percent of organisations have mechanisms to respond to anonymous whistleblowing, only 16 percent had any policy for ensuring adequate compensation for whistleblowers.

This is a major issue, given many whistleblowers experience reprisals and career disruption as a result of bringing wrongdoing to light, and then have to fight their case before the Fair Work Commission. The research also highlighted a disconnect between the workplace and the law.

While workplace policies encourage anonymous whistleblowing, Australia's Corporations Act protects only whistleblowers that are willing to identify themselves.

How Australian Law Compares

The issue of anonymity is a critical one for many whistleblowers, and it is now addressed in new Australian legislation, the Treasury Laws Amendment (Whistleblowers) Bill, which aims to create a single whistleblower protection regime in the Corporations Act.

The Australian whistleblowing legislation follows the model of the UK and other Commonwealth countries, such as Canada. It is very different from the US where there are two pieces of legislation: the False Claims Act that covers government contracts and was introduced to stop fraud against the Union Army during the Civil War, and more recent corporate legislation under the 2010 Dodd-Frank reforms, which followed the global financial crisis (GFC).

In the US, a cornerstone of the later legislation is a compensation scheme where whistleblowers are awarded a percentage of any fines imposed by the courts, usually set at between 10 and 30 percent.

Under this legislation, administered by the Office of the Whistleblower operating under the Securities and Exchange Commission (SEC), US$252 million has been paid out to 53 whistleblowers in the last seven years. Whistleblowers can also remain anonymous and, according to US lawyer Mary Inman, there are several examples where a whistleblower has anonymously reported his or her employer, been awarded compensation, and is still working in the organisation.

The #METOO Movement

Inman is a partner in US law firm Constantine Cannon, and has been representing whistleblowers for more than 20 years. In March 2018, Constantine Cannon announced that two of its clients would receive more than US$1.13 million for information they provided to the US Government in its criminal case against Takata, the now bankrupt maker of defective car airbags that caused the deaths of 22 people.

"I see that we are in an unprecedented moment with whistleblowing right now," Inman says. "You look at the #MeToo movement on sexual harassment, and the grassroots movement of young activists against gun laws in the US, and I see whistleblowing in that context."

Inman recently moved to London to head up her firm's international whistleblower practice because the US laws are also accessible to citizens of other countries with information about

US-listed companies. The SEC whistleblower program receives around 4000 submissions a year, including a significant percentage from outside the US; notably from the UK, Canada and Australia.

"I feel that the SEC is, in my estimation, the best whistleblower program and it's the model that other programs should be aspiring to," Inman says. "That is because it has the trifecta of protections. It has incentives, anonymity and it has protection against retaliation. Right now, it is the pinnacle."

Inman says the SEC has also been "incredibly aggressive" in pursuing the legislation, and penalising companies that have been trying to "chill" whistleblowers from coming forward. Some employers, she says, will write clauses into severance agreements so that if people leave the organisation, they give up their right to a whistleblowing reward. Many of these employers have been fined by the SEC for trying to "work around the program."

Rewarding Those Who Speak Up

Inman recognises that the major difference between US whistleblower laws and those in other countries, such as Australia, is the issue of compensation, but she believes the international tide is turning towards the US model.

"I know that Americans are seen as litigious and mercenary, and the fear is that you incentivise people for the wrong reasons," she says. "In Australia and [other] Commonwealth countries, the idea is that you should blow the whistle because it's the right thing to do, not because you need a financial incentive.

"However, I think people understand the reward is there less as a bounty and more as a safety net because of the repercussions that whistleblowers can suffer, such as being 'blackballed' or jeopardising their career."

Most American whistleblowers try to fix the issue from within their organisation before going straight to the regulator, suggesting that the legislation is working as intended. "If people are so anxious to get the money they will skip and bypass internal reporting, but the data shows that fewer than 3 percent of people do that," Inman says. "Only when they are rebuffed by their employer do they then go ahead with the whistleblower program."

The Morality of Receiving Money

Woodford, however, does not agree with a compensation system, believing it "undermines the morality of the whistleblower model." "I don't think that it is right to become a lottery winner for being a whistleblower—it is distasteful and disproportionate and gives whistleblowing a bad name," he insists.

"I think that whistleblowers should be protected and there should be a process of compensation if they have been wronged or damaged, but the law should look at each case as it stands."

Mansotte is also against a US-style compensation system, arguing that it would do "a lot of damage" to the image of whistleblowers.

"It is sending the wrong message to everybody that, yes, you can retire early and win the lottery," he says. "The danger is that people will just sniff around to find a rat they can expose and then retire."

For another side of the argument, look no further than Addison's story, which is an example of how financial ruin and the loss of a career besets many whistleblowers. Addison blew the whistle on her employer, Leisurenet, in 2000 after tipping off authorities to an elaborate fraud perpetrated by the company's two founders and joint chief executives.

Although the investigation began swiftly and prompted the collapse of the company, it wasn't until 2007 that the perpetrators were sentenced, and they only went to jail in 2011. Meanwhile, in 2001 Addison fled South Africa in fear for her life and obtained a job as treasurer at the Virgin Group in London.

Her past followed her, however, as Virgin entered into negotiations with Leisurenet to buy its assets. In the midst of this process Addison was fired, without explanation, six months into her new UK-based job.

"I was marched off the premises like a criminal, and had no rights to challenge this under UK laws," she says. "The Leisurenet enquiry had just got going in South Africa when Virgin was negotiating, so I was collateral damage to the negotiations because Virgin wanted to do business with the two people I had blown the whistle on."

Finding another job in finance in the UK proved impossible as recruiters became wary of putting her name forward because she had been let go by Virgin after only six months. One told her that he had googled her and seen that she had been treasurer of a company that was in liquidation, "which didn't look so good."

Another said that his recruitment firm did not want to compromise its relationships with clients by putting her forward. "The outcome for me was horrendous," Addison says. "I ended up squatting and begging on the streets, with my 12-year-old son."

Bouncing Back

After reinventing her career with her SpeakOut SpeakUp consultancy, Addison has a different perspective on whistleblowing and what advocacy can achieve. "The world has shifted in the last 12 to 18 months, and I see whistleblowers in South Africa speaking out on social media, which is incredibly brave," she says. "Now it is about empowering people to have courageous conversations, and to speak up before things start moving down that slippery slope.

"Whistleblowers are outliers, and I understand why they have been treated the way they have been, but we now are finding another way which educates people that while loyalty to the company is a good value to have, sometimes in certain contexts you have to put fairness above it."

Addison started work at the company which became Leisurenet in 1993, and soon observed "small ethical lapses" that over time evolved into illegality.

"I spoke out in 2000, but by then it was far too late," she says. "By that time the misconduct had been entrenched as business-as-normal, and it is difficult to blow the whistle on something that is the norm."

Tougher legislation, she says, is only one part of the required response. The ideal is one where employees feel able to speak up to organisations which, in turn, listen and take action before aberrant behaviour escalates, without retribution and "shooting the messenger."

In that world, whistleblowers won't need their #MeToo moment, but we're not there yet.

New Laws for Australia

The Australian Treasury Laws Amendment (Whistleblowers) Bill came into effect on 1 July 2018. It was introduced into Federal Parliament in December 2017 with the aim of creating a single protection regime, and it updates Australia's first whistleblower legislation, under the Corporations Act, which dates back to 2004.

Under the new legislation:

- Protection is extended to former officers, employees and suppliers, as well as associates of the entity and family members of employees.
- Public companies and large private companies are required to have a whistleblower policy or face a financial fine.
- Disclosures can be anonymous and immunities can be extended to whistleblowers.
- Fines of up to A$1 million can be imposed on corporations and up to A$200,000 on individuals who breach a whistleblower's anonymity or who threaten or victimise a whistleblower.
- Whistleblowers will be able to make protected disclosures to journalists and politicians if they have already made a disclosure to a "whistleblower disclosee" (which might be ASIC, APRA, the AFP, the ATO, or someone in the organisation authorised to receive disclosures, such as an auditor, actuary, director, or senior manager) and if there is a risk of serious harm if information is not acted on

immediately. To qualify for protection under this provision, however, they will first have to inform a (relevant) regulator or enforcement body.

• Whistleblowers will have the right to seek compensation for reprisals. Courts will be required to preserve and protect a whistleblower's identity, unless it is in the interest of justice to do otherwise.

What Should a Whistleblower Policy Include?

For whistleblowing to be effective in ending wrongdoing and protecting the whistleblower, it has to be viewed not as betrayal or disloyalty to an organisation, but as a service to society.

Here are four points any organisation should consider when creating or revising a whistleblower policy.

Organisational Responsibilty

Organisations should have robust internal whistleblowing processes, involving third parties retained specifically for this purpose. Employees must feel that they can come forward and report any suspected wrongdoing without fear of retribution or retaliation. If the organisation is unresponsive or the process is unsatisfactory, whistleblowers must then have a clear channel for reporting wrongdoing to regulators or law enforcement.

Anonymity

The US system allows for anonymous reporting, as does the new Australian legislation. Many potential whistleblowers remain silent for fear of being identified. The Whispli solution allows for anonymous two-way communication between whistleblowers and investigators.

Whistleblower Protection

Many whistleblowers have lost their jobs and careers because of speaking out. Anonymity is one protection, but in cases where the whistleblower is identified, they must be guaranteed freedom from retribution and punishment. In some jurisdictions, the onus is on the whistleblower to pursue justice through labour laws. This is not best practice.

Compensation

This is the most controversial issue in whistleblowing. In the US under the Dodd-Frank Wall Street Reform and Consumer Protection Act, whistleblowers receive a reward of up to 30 percent of fines levied. While proponents of the US approach claim it is world's best practice, other jurisdictions such as Australia have yet to go down the same path of compensation formulas.

Financial Incentives Prompt Disclosures of Fraud

Paolo Buccirossi, Giovanni Immordino, and Giancarlo Spagnolo

Paolo Buccirossi is affiliated with the Laboratorio di economia, antitrust, regolamentazione (LEAR). Giovanni Immordino is associated with the University of Salerno's Centre for Studies in Economics and Finance (CSEF). Giancarlo Spagnolo is affiliated with the Stockholm School of Economics.

Corporate fraud is endemic. Dyck et al. (2013) estimated that between 1996 and 2004, about 15% of large publicly traded US corporations engaged in fraud. These crimes have an expected cost of $380 billion. Following corporate scandals at Enron, Parmalat, Worldcom, Siemens, Madoff, Volkswagen, and the Libor and Forex manipulation schemes, some European governments are debating whether to follow the US and introduce financial rewards for whistleblowers who report corporate crime to the authorities.

Corporate whistleblowers are usually employees. They often report the problem externally only after they report it internally and are ignored, sanctioned or harassed by their superiors. After blowing the whistle they are often subjected to unverifiable internal retaliation. Realising this, in recent years the US authorities have increased the use of financial rewards for whistleblowers, similar to the rewards that have been used since the US civil war for rooting out fraud in federal contracts (Nyerod and Spagnolo 2017).

Discovering crimes by eliciting existing information from witnesses or accomplices may be more efficient than finding new information through an investigation. If it is difficult to protect whistleblowers from retaliation, and if retaliation against

"Whistleblower rewards, false reports, and corporate fraud," by Paolo Buccirossi, Giovanni Immordino, Giancarlo Spagnolo, October 11, 2017. ©VoxEU.org. https://voxeu.org/article/effective-rewards-whistleblowing.

whistleblowers is difficult for a court to ascertain, financial rewards for whistleblowers can be seen as compensation. In addition, if they are large enough, rewards provide strong incentives to report corporate infringement.

European authorities are still wary of the explicit, structured financial incentives for whistleblowers that are increasingly popular with US enforcement agencies. This is partly because they fear large incentives lead to unintended harmful consequences when management is poor or there is a lack of administrative capacity, and also because historically this type of incentive was used by authoritarian regimes against internal opponents. For these reasons, US enforcement practices may not be viable in Europe.

The origin of the animosity to rewards for whistleblowers from corporate lawyers and some of the regulatory authorities in Europe, however, is less clear. For example, in 2014 the two main UK financial market watchdogs—the Prudential Regulation Authority of the Bank of England and the Financial Conduct Authority—wrote a joint response to a request for opinion from the Parliamentary Committee on Banking Standards. "There is as yet no empirical evidence of incentives leading to an increase in the number or quality of disclosures received by the regulators," it said.

This is incorrect. Dyck et al. showed empirically that whistleblower rewards under the False Claim Act in the US were highly effective in encouraging employees to blow the whistle. Engstrom offered additional empirical evidence of positive effects of this whistleblower reward system. Baloria et al. showed that opposition to whistleblower rewards came mostly from companies with poor corporate governance.

More recently, Wilde provided evidence that whistleblowing deters financial misreporting and tax aggressiveness. Call et al. found that, when whistleblowers provide evidence in financial misrepresentation enforcement actions, proceedings begin sooner, there are higher monetary sanctions for the guilty firm, there is a higher likelihood that criminal sanctions are imposed, and when executives are convicted they spend more time in jail.

Opponents nevertheless claim that these schemes induce reports based on false or fabricated information. Evidence from the US, however, suggests that this has not been a major problem. US agencies argue that, when appropriately designed and managed, they both increase crime detection rates and largely pay for their administration costs.

A Model of Whistleblower Incentives

In recent work, we develop a model of the interaction between rewards for whistleblowers, sanctions for fraudulently reporting false or fabricated information, judicial errors, and standards of proof in two types of court case (one based on a whistleblower's allegations, and the following one, typically neglected, for defamation or perjury against a whistleblower who loses the first case).

The policy debate typically neglects to consider that schemes can be designed in many ways, and that every legal system already has tools in place that are specifically designed to prevent fraudulent claims based on false information, such as defamation and perjury laws. Therefore the risk of an increase in false or fabricated claims can be reduced by strengthening these tools, rather than by giving up on the potential of whistleblower rewards.

The risk that high-powered incentives lead to many fabricated accusations can be controlled directly through severe sanctions against defamation, perjury and information fabrication. It could also be controlled by the adoption of a stricter standard of proof for information provided by witnesses who stand to gain from a conviction. This may reduce the incentive to forge information linked to rewards, but at the cost of a lower conviction rate. Alternatively, the risk of fabrication could also be reduced by lowering or capping rewards for whistleblowers. But all these strategies have costs, because they would mean weaker enforcement, and so reduce the deterrent effect on corporate fraud.

Therefore, the optimal policy will likely involve a mix of strategies. Variation in the efficiency and precision of legal systems also means that different policies may be optimal in different institutional environments.

- We discover that to design an effective reward programme, in which whistleblowers do not deliberately present false claims but do file reports when a firm misbehaves, it is crucial to find an optimal balance between the reward offered to successful whistleblowers and the sanctions against those convicted for knowingly reporting false information. Given other parameters, a balanced ratio between these two parameters leads to an optimal programme, suggesting that severe sanctions against whistleblowers convicted for forging information are necessary to compensate for large rewards, and vice versa.

- Because retaliation from employers is possible, and not all forms of retaliation can be observed by a court, we show that there is a minimum size of reward, below which whistleblowing will not take place at all, that is independent of the ratio of sanctions and rewards. If the risk is high that a firm will retaliate, and the weaker the whistleblower protection, any reward must also substantially exceed the sanction imposed on a mendacious whistleblower.

- An overly strict standard of proof, with very few false positives and therefore many false negatives, induces whistleblowers to never report and the firm to always commit wrongdoing. Similarly, when the standard of proof is too low, the many false positives induce whistleblowers to always blow the whistle, whether or not the firm is guilty. The standard of proof must therefore be chosen with due care to avoid turning these schemes into failures.

- We find that when the top management is involved in the wrongdoing, internal whistleblower channels can be easily misused to undermine external whistleblower channels. They allow management to bribe the employee that reports internally, so that the information does not reach law enforcement agencies. As a consequence, the programmes should not require the whistleblower to first report internally.

- Improving the accuracy of courts reduces both types of error, and is the only policy with unambiguously positive effects. This policy is costly, but a well-functioning whistleblower reward scheme may reduce detection and prosecution costs and at the same time increase recoveries, thereby compensating for the costs of increased accuracy.

Whistleblower Schemes Are Useful Instruments

From a short-run perspective, therefore, our results imply that whistleblowing reward schemes are useful instruments that can be effectively designed and administered—and should therefore be welcome if there is interest and political will to fight corporate misbehavior, provided the court system is sufficiently precise. Our results also imply that, in environments with weak institutions, where court precision and administrative capabilities are low, these tools are likely not to perform as one would hope. In this case, they should be avoided.

To Combat Profitable Fraud, Significant Rewards Must Be Offered

Daniel Van Schooten

Daniel Van Schooten is an investigator with the Project on Government Oversight (POGO). He has conducted investigations and drafted reports on whistleblowing since 2015.

Potential changes to the False Claims Act (FCA), a law that incentivizes whistleblowers to sue those that defraud the government, fell flat at a House Judiciary subcommittee hearing late last month. While everyone at the hearing agreed that prevention of fraud is ideal, industry representatives faced strong resistance when they argued that the government should reduce the punishments for fraudulent companies that have compliance systems in place. The majority of the conversation centered on that argument, but other potential changes referenced in opening statements and written testimony included forcing whistleblowers to report fraud to their boss before being able to file a lawsuit and prohibiting the government from debarring corporations that self-report fraud.

Subcommittee on the Constitution and Civil Justice Chairman Trent Franks (R-AZ) opened the hearing by acknowledging the success of the FCA in recovering huge sums of money—over $3 billion each year for the past six years. But he also pointed out that there was room for improvement, citing a 2015 Government Accountability Office report that found that $125 billion in improper payments had been made in 2014. Used in this context, that number can be somewhat misleading, as it includes any payments that "should not have been made or that were made in an incorrect amount," whether it is due to contractors deliberately defrauding the government or unintentional government errors.

"Challenge to False Claims Act Falls Flat at House Hearing," by Daniel Van Schooten, Project On Government Oversight, May 10, 2016. https://www.pogo.org/analysis/2016/05/challenge-to-false-claims-act-falls-flat-at-house-hearing/. Reprinted by permission.

Ranking Member Steve Cohen (D-TN) defended the FCA as is, vigorously attacking various proposals that had been made to restrict *qui tam* lawsuits, a provision in the FCA that allows whistleblowers to sue on behalf of the government and claim part of the recovery. With almost 70 percent of all FCA recoveries originating with *qui tam* lawsuits, Cohen advocated for protecting and encouraging whistleblowers to come forward. Proposals to reduce the whistleblower's share of the damages or to require whistleblowers to meet a restrictively high standard of proof, he stated, would demotivate the very whistleblowers the law's effectiveness relies on. However, he saw the most blatant threat to the effectiveness of the FCA to be the idea that whistleblowers should be required to report fraud to their supervisors before being able to file a lawsuit. "Great idea, you gotta go tell your boss that he's a crook and he's gonna be caught and exposed... That's a great way to inhibit the people from coming forward—quieting the whistle," Cohen said during his opening statement.

During witness testimony, Dennis Burke, President of the Good Shepherd Health Care System, testified that from 2003 to 2006 his organization was subjected to $1 million in legal costs due to a baseless whistleblower lawsuit. He used this example to push for greater restrictions on whistleblowers filing *qui tam* lawsuits. While this type of situation is concerning, it is also rare. Protections exist for organizations that have been falsely accused, and the fact that opponents of the law placed a ten-year-old story in the spotlight is telling. This was sharply contrasted by the prime example of effective whistleblower-led lawsuits, where defenders of the FCA's *qui tam* provisions had to go back just one day to find a *qui tam* lawsuit that culminated in a headline-making $785 million fraud settlement from pharmaceutical giant Pfizer.

Other witnesses also pushed for reduced corporate liability. Reducing the liability of companies with strong compliance systems in place, they argued, would incentivize companies to create a culture of integrity that would prevent future fraud. Neil Getnick,

Chairman of Taxpayers Against Fraud Education Fund, attacked that proposal, labeling it a "pie-in-the-sky idea with no specifics."

> Allowing companies to escape or face reduced liability from FCA actions because they have "checked the boxes" on how to establish a compliance program is doomed to fail. It will merely encourage companies to game this new compliance regime the same way they game contract and regulatory requirements. Such gaming does not reduce fraud; it enables fraud.

Fraud is profitable, and those that engage in it are unlikely to stop, especially if the penalties are reduced for self-disclosure. Without the threat of *qui tam* lawsuits, there is nothing to stop companies from continuing to defraud the government, rather than self-disclosing fraud and subjecting themselves to some form of punishment, reduced or not. Furthermore, the FCA "already contains a provision that allows corporations to reduce their liability by one-third if they self-report a fraud within thirty days of becoming aware of it," Getnick stated in his written testimony. "This is a rarely used provision, and repeat FCA scofflaws abound."

The statistics back up the importance of preserving the FCA. Over $3.5 billion was recovered under the False Claims Act in 2015 alone, with well over $48 billion recovered over the life of the program. *Qui tam* cases are responsible for recovering almost 70 percent of the $48 billion recovered. If we restrict the ability of whistleblowers to file cases against their employers, we are sure to see that number fall dramatically.

Reform of the False Claims Act Needed Due to High Costs

Gregory Klass and Michael Holt

Gregory Klass and Michael Holt are both affiliates of Georgetown University's Law Center. Professor Klass has published various articles on law and fraud, and their collaborative work focuses on the specifics of the False Claims Act.

A mong the core doctrines of US contract law is that there are no punitive damages for a mere breach of contract. In fact, in many jurisdictions, a party can lie about or cover up a breach without risking punitive damages in fraud, under the rule that a breach cannot support an action for fraud. But government contracts are different. The False Claims Act (FCA) expressly prohibits government contractors from submitting "a false record or statement" material to a claim for payment. And under the judicially created doctrine of implied certification, a mere request for payment implicitly represents material compliance with the contract, as well as relevant statutes and regulations. As a result, a government contractor who requests payment without disclosing a known material breach can violate the FCA, triggering treble damages and fines of between $5,000 and $10,000 for each payment request. Whereas between private parties even an express lie about performance will often go unpunished, the mere request for payment by a noncompliant government contractor can result in significant legal liability.

Although the implied certification doctrine is radical from the perspective of "normal" contract law, contract scholars have to date paid scant attention to it. The neglect is all the more remarkable given the dollar amounts at stake. The Department of Justice reports that *qui tam* plaintiffs alone filed over 300 False Claims Act actions

"Implied Certification under the False Claims Act," by Gregory Klass and Michael Holt, Georgetown University Law Center, 2011.

per year in each of the past fifteen years. In all but one of the last ten years, settlements and judgments under the FCA have totaled over $1 billion. In 2010, the Government initiated 138 cases and recovered over $620 million, while *qui tam* plaintiffs filed 574 suits and recovered nearly $2.5 billion in settlements and judgments. While the Department of Justice does not disaggregate claims of implied certification, individual implied-certification cases have resulted in awards upwards of $99 million. Twenty-seven states, the District of Columbia, and many cities have analogous statutes. And the Securities and Exchange Commission, in response to high-profile frauds by members of the securities industry, has recently implemented enhanced whistleblower provisions modeled after the FCA. The scholarly inattention to the implied certification doctrine is also remarkable given the confusion in the case law. Circuits are today split on implied certification. Several have expressly declined to recognize the doctrine. Those that have allowed claims of implied certification differ on the scope of the rule.

This article aims to develop a theory of implied certification under the False Claims Act and to recommend a way forward for both courts and contracting agencies. Our theory has two parts. First, we argue that the FCA as a whole is designed to enable the Government to contract for information about performance—information for which the Government has a special need. This locates the FCA within the broader theory of contractual duties to cooperate in recovery for breach. Second, we argue that the implied certification rule is best understood as a dual interpretive default. Most obviously, the rule establishes a default interpretation of government contractors' claims for payment: absent a statement to the contrary, the request represents material compliance with the contract and with relevant statutes and regulations. Because parties could contract around that claim default, the implied certification rule is also a contractual default: claims for payment are interpreted in accordance with the first default only if the parties have not provided otherwise in their contract.

This theoretical framework allows us to systematically identify and evaluate the costs and benefits of the implied certification rule. Applying Ian Ayres and Robert Gertner's theory of interpretive defaults, we argue that the default interpretation of a claim as representing material compliance is both majoritarian and information forcing. It is majoritarian because, one hopes, most government contractors who request payment are in material compliance and so would want to make the representation. It is information forcing because the rule gives contractors in breach a new reason to share that fact. We also argue that the certification default is separately justified by the special ethical obligations of government contractors. Contractors who have knowingly and materially breached their contract with the Government or violated relevant statutes and regulations should disclose that fact before requesting payment.

But implied certification also has its costs. The certification default lowers the pleading bar, making it easier for a frivolous *qui tam* lawsuit to survive a motion to dismiss. And it threatens to extend FCA liability to contractor duties that are more effectively monitored and enforced in other ways. These costs suggest some advantage of forcing the Government to expressly contract for implied certification. Without implied certification as the contractual default, contracting agencies might be more likely to evaluate where FCA liability is beneficial and to craft express certification requirements accordingly. The last advantage, however, assumes a certain level of care and competence in contracting agencies. A more jaundiced view suggests an institutional-competence argument for the contractual default: the implied certification rule extends the FCA's protections to reach transactions in which the contracting agency has erroneously failed to require express certifications of compliance.

Our dual-default theory of the implied certification rule results in practical recommendations for both courts and contracting agencies. Courts that have not yet recognized implied certification should do so, and we propose a new rule for deciding implied certification cases. Under this rule, the fact that a contract, statute, or regulation conditions either participation in or payment for a contract on compliance with it creates a prima facie case that a claim for payment represented such compliance, shifting the burden to the defendant to show that FCA liability would interfere with other regulatory monitoring and enforcement mechanisms. This rule balances the competing costs and benefits of implied certification and resolves several open questions in the implied certification jurisprudence. While it has yet to be articulated by any court, the rule finds support in the FCA case law.

In a first-best world, there would be no need for implied certification. Agencies at the time of contracting would weigh the costs and benefits of certification backed by the FCA, and require that contractors expressly certify compliance with only those duties where FCA certification would be advantageous. But even with implied certification, contracting agencies can take steps to approximate first-best results. Herein lies the benefit of identifying the rule as a contractual default. Agencies can and should write their contracts to require express certification of compliance with those duties for which FCA liability makes sense. And they should expressly contract out of implied certification of compliance with duties that are better enforced by other regulatory mechanisms.

[...]

Implied Certification of Compliance

[...]

Those schooled in the theory of efficient breach might worry that increased FCA liability threatens to undermine the expectation measure of damages. Supercompensatory awards such as the FCA's treble damages and per-claim fines, the objection goes, will tend to discourage efficient breaches, and the Government will ultimately pay for that efficiency loss. A contractor that knows that, if its costs of performance go up or if a better opportunity appears, it will not have the option of breaching and paying damages will charge the

Government a higher price for its goods or services. That higher price will not correspond to a better product, but will reflect the reduced value that the transaction is expected to generate. The costs to contractors of expanded FCA liability will be passed on to the Government.

This worry rests on two mistakes. First, it neglects the simplifying assumptions of the efficient breach theory: that the nonbreaching party is aware of the breach and that the transaction costs of awarding expectation damages are less than it would cost the parties to negotiate a release. The FCA comes into play only when these simplifying assumptions do not hold. Under the implied certification rule, a contractor has violated the FCA only if the Government paid a claim in ignorance of a material breach, and then only because the contractor breached its duty to cooperate by failing to inform the Government of its nonperformance. Without knowledge of the breach, the Government will not sue for expectation damages. Far from threatening efficient breach, the duties to cooperate that the FCA enforces are designed to secure the conditions that make efficient breach possible.

Second, the efficient breach theory assumes that the only costs of a breach are monetizable losses suffered by the nonbreaching party. As we have already observed, government contracts often include material terms—statutory or regulatory compliance, ownership requirements, adherence to labor and hiring standards— that are not designed solely to increase the value of the goods or services provided. Because the breach of such a term does not impose a direct financial loss on the Government, it is difficult to judge when that breach is efficient. More to the point, there is no guarantee that the expectation measure will force the breaching party to internalize the social costs of such violations, though those social costs are precisely the reason the Government chose to include the term in the contract.

[...]

Conclusion

Implied certification of post-formation compliance plays an important role in the regulation of government contracts. By effectively imposing on contractors a duty to disclose material breaches, implied certification addresses the Government's difficulties in monitoring performance and recognizes the special ethical obligations that attach to government contracts. As a contractual default, the rule also addresses the problems of agency capture and competence in the contracting process, making it more likely that the protections of the False Claims Act will reach contractors who attempt to take advantage of lax government oversight. In practice, courts have applied the doctrine in a way that generally prevents interference with other regulatory mechanisms and protects contractors against frivolous *qui tam* lawsuits. And because the rule is a mere default, it leaves room for contracting agencies to further specify defaults and disclosure duties in individual transactions.

The best rule for when a claim for payment implicitly represents performance lies somewhere between the rules in *Ab-Tech* and in *Mikes*. The fact that compliance with a contract term, statute, or regulation is a condition of payment for or participation in a government contract should create a strong legal presumption that a claim for payment under the contract implicitly represents such compliance. That presumption should be rebutted only if a defendant can show that FCA liability would interfere with other regulatory mechanisms. Such a showing is difficult if not impossible where the agency or legislature has expressly provided that compliance is a condition of payment. It is easier where compliance is a condition only of participation in the transaction where the condition is implicit, or where the rule gives government decision makers discretion to pay despite a breach or violation.

Even under our more tailored rule, implied certification is not without its costs. This is why we would welcome greater agency attention to certification in the drafting of contracts. We also note that many of the costs of implied certification of compliance come not from the rule itself, but from other aspects of the False Claims Act. We have already described how the availability of *qui tam* actions magnifies the costs of implied certification. While *qui tam* actions are an essential part of the FCA's architecture, Congress might consider raising the bar for claims of implied certification in cases where the Government elects not to appear. Also relevant in this respect are the FCA's mandatory penalties, particularly the $5,000 to $10,000 per-claim fines. In cases involving factual falsehoods—claims for goods or services not provided—those fines bear some relation to the underlying wrong. Each claim is another lie. This is not so in cases involving legal falsehoods, expressed or implied. Here the underlying wrong is the false certification or undisclosed violation. The seriousness of such a lie or nondisclosure bears no relationship to the number of times the contractor billed the Government for goods or services rendered. The multiplying effect of per-claim fines further increases the potential costs of frivolous litigation and the potential interference of the FCA with other regulatory mechanisms. The act's remedial structure is another area that might benefit from legislative attention.

Finally, and more generally, Congress should consider amending the False Claims Act to expressly recognize and regularize implied certification. Section 3729(a)(1)(G), which authorizes reverse FCA claims, already includes such language. In addition to imposing liability on a contractor who "knowingly makes, uses, or causes to be made or used, a false record or statement"—the same language as that in section (1)(B)—section (1)(G) imposes liability on one who "knowingly conceals or knowingly and improperly avoids or decreases an obligation to pay or transmit money or property to the Government." While this formulation is not perfect, by adding some such language to section (1)(B) Congress could provide clearer statutory authority for the implied certification doctrine.

[...]

Paying Whistleblowers Does Not Help in Every Situation

Lloyd Hitoshi Mayer

Lloyd Hitoshi Mayer is a professor at Notre Dame Law School. He teaches classes on not-for-profit organizations, business enterprise taxation, election law, and professional responsibility.

Recent events have highlighted the difficulties the Internal Revenue Service (IRS) faces when attempting to ensure that purportedly tax-exempt organizations do in fact qualify for that status. These problems go much deeper than a group of IRS employees subjecting certain organizations to greater scrutiny based on their political leanings. For decades, members of the public, the media, the academy, and Congress have criticized the limited ability of the IRS to ensure that organizations claiming exemption from federal income tax in fact deserve that categorization. Yet, examples of IRS failings in this area continue to arise with depressing frequency despite numerous suggestions for improvement and various congressional and agency initiatives. This is consistent with the major difficulties faced by the IRS as a whole and discussed by other presenters at this symposium. As detailed in this article, these difficulties have rendered the IRS unable to keep pace with the growth of the exempt organizations sector over the past 40 years.

One of the latest such initiatives suggests a new approach, however. In 2014, the IRS introduced the much shorter and simpler Form 1023-EZ application for nonprofit organizations that claim exempt charitable status and expect to have only modest financial resources, accompanied by faster procedures for handling all applications for recognition of exemption. These innovations represent the first significant, permanent reduction in the level of oversight the IRS provides in this area since the introduction of the Form 990-EZ, a shorter version of the annual information return required for most exempt organizations. It is arguable, however, whether a reduction of oversight is in fact prudent and whether other reductions might also be advisable. [...] This article concludes that while marginal improvements in oversight are possible, there is no silver bullet to counter the IRS's growing inability to oversee this area.

[...]

Modifying Oversight

This Part [...] considers whether there are currently promising candidates for improving oversight in light of the resource constraints the IRS faces, drawing on the extensive literature addressing tax law compliance more generally. This consideration includes describing the recent IRS initiatives to reduce oversight at the application stage and discussing how best to evaluate the effects of such changes.

[...]

Methods Unlikely to Significantly Improve Oversight

Some of the methods proposed to aid compliance with the federal tax laws are generally a poor fit for exempt organizations. For example, increasing the regulation of or penalties on gatekeepers such as lawyers and accountants is unlikely to be particularly helpful. This is both because many exempt organizations do not use such gatekeepers and because there is evidence that the exempt organizations most likely to have the resources to engage such gatekeepers, such as colleges, universities, and hospitals, generally have a high level of compliance with the applicable federal tax laws. Similarly, increasing the penalties for noncompliance imposed on the organizations or their managers would only enhance compliance if the organizations and their leaders are aware of those costs and believe there is a significant risk of discovery of non-compliance. None of these facts appear to exist with respect to most exempt organizations; most such organizations lack expert advisors to inform them about potential penalties, usually because of resource constraints, and the current examination rate, and thus the risk of discovery is—and is known to be—very low.

Rewarding whistleblowers and encouraging private enforcement actions through enabling *qui tam* lawsuits are alternative methods for enhancing compliance with the federal tax laws without requiring increased governmental resources, since they enlist private parties to improve compliance. The success of the existing federal tax whistleblowing program has been relatively limited, however, and has not generated much interest with respect to exempt organizations. Furthermore, rewards for whistleblowers (and *qui tam* suit filers) are usually a portion of the tax revenue collected as a result, which would not be particularly effective with respect to exempt organizations. Insiders at charities and other exempt organizations may also be less inclined to engage in whistleblowing than employees of for-profit companies because of the potential harm to their organization's mission and those who benefit from its activities. Finally, the exempt organizations area may be particularly vulnerable to damaging harassment if such methods are available, given the controversial nature of some exempt organizations and their usually limited financial resources to defend themselves against false accusations.

[...]

Methods with the Potential to Significantly Improve Oversight

Several methods show more promise, however. The IRS has already implemented one set of such methods by introducing procedures and a new form to streamline the application process for organizations seeking recognition of exempt status. Another set of such methods is greater reliance on resource-intensive examination techniques, such as correspondence audits, no-contact review of operations procedures, and the use of compliance data to better target examinations. A third set of such methods is designed to improve disclosure and transparency to enhance media and public input with respect to exempt organizations, including during both the application and examination processes. A final promising method would be requiring increased electronic filing.

[...]

Conclusion

The IRS oversight of exempt organizations with respect to their compliance with applicable federal tax laws has reached a breaking point. Absent significant changes, the public's confidence both in the ability of the IRS to provide such oversight and in the good behavior of exempt organizations themselves will almost certainly continue to decline. And that decline may soon reach a point, if it has not already, that threatens both the IRS's ability to fulfill its primary, revenue-collecting responsibilities and the public support on which most exempt organizations rely.

Even with its current resources and with no changes in the applicable substantive law, there are several ways in which the IRS could improve its oversight of exempt organizations. These ways include continuing to use streamlined application procedures, increasing the efficiency of the examination process, ensuring greater disclosure of relevant information, and expanding electronic filing requirements. Particularly if enacted together and carefully evaluated and recalibrated as necessary to maximize their impact on compliance, these methods have the potential to help the IRS do more with less.

But given the resource constraints faced by the IRS and the continuing growth of the exempt organization sector, it is unlikely that these methods will be sufficient to attain an acceptable level of oversight for exempt organizations. The time is therefore ripe to consider bolder but riskier proposals to shift the oversight of exempt organizations outside of the IRS. While a new federal agency has certain advantages, a new self-regulatory body that operates under the close supervision of the IRS appears to be a significantly better candidate for obtaining funding and freedom needed to substantially increase this oversight and therefore compliance with the federal tax laws applicable to exempt organizations. While the risks of moving this mature regulatory role out of the federal government are substantial and not completely known, such that any such move would require careful consideration of what functions would move out of the IRS, how such a transition would be sequenced, and how it would be evaluated, it is time to pursue this option.

[...]

CHAPTER 4

Is Whistleblowing the Best Way to Limit Corruption?

Various Acts Attempt to Prevent Wrongdoing

Shannon Kay Quigley

Shannon Kay Quigley studied law at the Santa Clara University School of Law.

Whistleblowing occurs when an employee attempts to "blow the whistle" and expose a wrongdoing within a corporation or organization. Whistleblowing may occur internally, when an employee contacts a manager or a supervisor, or externally, when an employee reports to a government agency or media representative. The public has deemed some whistleblowers the "voices of reason" who act to protect the public. Though a few whistleblowers succeed in identifying and stopping fraud, most employees with personal knowledge of corruption fail to report the information, and the fraud remains undiscovered. To promote whistleblowing to the government, several federal statutes incorporate "bounty" provisions, or monetary incentives, for whistleblowers to report valuable information. Many employees compare the monetary incentives to the risk of retaliation by co-workers and employers who brand the whistleblower a *snitch,* an *informer,* or worse, a *traitor.* In order to protect whistleblowers from such reprisals, statutes often contain retaliation provisions that forbid employers from firing employees for whistleblowing.

In a promise to "clean up" the financial services industry and the prevalent fraud, President Obama signed the Dodd- Frank Wall Street Reform and Consumer Protection Act (Dodd-Frank Act) in 2010. The Dodd-Frank Act provides monetary incentives for whistleblowers who report fraudulent corporate practices to the government. Yet eight years prior, Congress enacted the Sarbanes-Oxley Act to decrease fraudulent activities by requiring corporations

Shannon Kay Quigley, Comment, "Whistleblower Tug-of-War: Corporate Attempts to Secure Internal Reporting Procedures in the Face of External Monetary Incentives Provided by the Dodd-Frank Act," 52 Santa Clara L. Rev. 255 (2012). Available at: http://digitalcommons.law.scu.edu/lawreview/vol52/iss1/7

to construct internal reporting mechanisms. Congress designed these mechanisms to encourage employees to report fraud and promote corporate self-regulation. Corporations are still required to maintain the internal reporting mechanisms and compliance programs required by the Sarbanes-Oxley Act, even though the monetary incentives provided by the Dodd-Frank Act undermine the purpose of such programs. For example, a public accountant for a major corporation may discover information that implicates a manager in an act of fraud. On one hand, the accountant may report to the company and risk retaliation. On the other hand, the accountant could report to the government for a substantial reward and receive protection for their whistleblowing activities.

As of 2010, the Securities and Exchange Commission (SEC) has not granted a whistleblower award under the Dodd-Frank Act. However, the recent $96 million dollar award to Cheryl Eckard under a similar whistleblower provision, the False Claims Act, exasperated corporate concern of the potential impact created by external whistleblowing awards.

[...]

An Analysis of the Dodd-Frank Act

Corporations will only face an employee "tug-of-war" if the Dodd-Frank Act is successful at enticing employees to report to the SEC. If the possibility of a monetary award is too remote or the retaliation provisions are too narrow, an employee may feel more comfortable with an easy, self-explanatory corporate compliance program. However, if the Dodd-Frank Act successfully provides awards, the chain reaction could escalate the number of employees comfortable with whistleblowing to the SEC. In tough economic times, when employees fear losing their jobs, the effect of retaliation provisions is also essential to understanding an employee's willingness to betray the corporation and subject it to government involvement. Finally, an evaluation of the success of past federal statutes and the potential success of the Dodd-Frank Act is necessary to understanding the potential impact on compliance programs.

Whistleblower Incentives

A few statutes have recognized bounty provisions for whistleblowers. The Dodd-Frank Act is structurally similar to some of these provisions, but there are some major innovations that will affect the application and success of whistleblower awards. Several factors are necessary to determine the potential of the act based on the extent of the awards provided to potential whistleblower: (1) the scope of the statute, (2) the conditions necessary to qualify for a whistleblower award, (3) the certainty and the source of receiving an award, (4) the amount of the award and discretion of the agency, and (5) the anonymity of the whistleblower.

[…]

Sufficient Information

In order to recover an award under the Dodd-Frank Act the whistleblower must provide original information to the SEC. This provision is more restrictive than the FCA, which does not require the whistleblower to provide original information-it only requires the whistleblower to be the original source of information. In comparison, the Dodd-Frank Act proscribes that the information be "derived from the independent knowledge or analysis . . . not known to the Commission . . . and is not exclusively derived from . . . [a] hearing, audit, or investigation, or from the news media." Further, the original information requirement induces the corporation to self-report violations before the employee, because the whistleblower's information would no longer be "original" within the meaning of the Dodd-Frank Act. However, when pressed to report first, the company will have to distinguish information that is worth reporting from that of mere speculation in a short time period, and risk the threat of unnecessary government involvement should the report be unsubstantiated. Since the employee must provide critical original information to the government before the corporation informs the government, the act deters employees from alerting the corporation through internal compliance programs.

The Certainty of Receiving an Award

The Dodd-Frank Act creates uncertainty by limiting awards to successful prosecution and basing the payment on uncertain factors. The SEC must prosecute the violator and limit the whistleblower award to a percentage of the monetary sanctions "collected" from the particular action. Unlike other similar statutes that derive the whistleblower award from monetary penalties paid by the violator, the Dodd-Frank Act established the Securities and Exchange Commission Investor Protection Fund in the Treasury of the United States. This Fund pays the whistleblower award out of the money collected by the Commission in judicial actions— even if unrelated to the matter on which the award is based—and income recovered from the investment of the Fund. If the amount of the Fund is insufficient to cover the entire whistleblower award, "there shall be deposited into or credited to the Fund an amount equal to the unsatisfied portion of the award from any monetary sanctions collected by the Commission in the covered judicial or administrative action on which the award is based."

Therefore, the statutory language implies that the SEC must collect the monetary sanction prior to completing the unsatisfied remainder of the award. Even if the whistleblower obtained part of the award from the Fund, the remainder of the award is contingent on the SEC's ability to recover money from the violator. While the statutory language may concern a potential external whistleblower as to the certainty of the award, the fund currently has $451 million; thus, it is unlikely that whistleblowers will be concerned that the SEC will not collect the sanction from violator before awarding the whistleblower.

Determining the Amount of the Award

In determining the amount of an award, it is essential to provide the proper balance between encouraging whistleblowers to reveal the truth and not giving them an incentive to falsify a report of fraud. Exorbitant awards entice whistleblowers to provide information but may also create false whistleblowers; however, inconsequential awards will not provide the incentive necessary to encourage whistleblowers to overcome their fear of retaliation. "An informer would have little incentive to give original information, upon occasions at considerable personal risk, to officers of the United States if his compensation rested in the absolute discretion ...[or] in the whim of an [SEC] executive officer." The Act limits the discretion of the SEC to determine the amount of the award to 10%-30% of the monetary judgment. The Act also limits the SEC to specific criteria for determining the exact percentage of the award: the significance of the information to the judicial action, the degree of assistance, the interest of the Commission in deterring violations, and other relevant factors established by the Commission in rules or regulations. Limiting the SEC's discretion ensures that the award will be sufficient to motivate employees to reveal the truth, but not significant enough to encourage fabricated claims.

[...]

Successful Application of Past Whistleblower Acts

The Dodd-Frank Act is not revolutionary in providing whistleblower incentives, as other statutes such as the FCA, the Insider Trading Act, the Tax Relief Act, and other federal programs have provided comparable incentives. The economic and procedural details of each existing bounty program demonstrate the factors relevant to the specific program's success or failure. While there may be some minor structural differences between the Dodd-Frank Act and other statutes, the success of past provisions can serve as an indicator of the potential effect of the Dodd-Frank Act.

Since the enactment of the FCA in 1986, the Attorney General recovered approximately $24 billion in sanctions that resulted after whistleblowers provided information leading to the discovery of false claims. In 2009, the federal government recovered $2.4 billion dollars from the FCA; nearly $2 billion resulted from *qui tam* actions and $255 million was awarded to *qui tam* plaintiffs. While this is a great indicator of the potential success of a whistleblower statute, the Dodd-Frank Act is more structurally limited than the broad language of the FCA.

[...]

Effective Compliance Programs for Corporations Responding to External Incentives of the Dodd-Frank Act

Despite some drawbacks and uncertainties concerning the Dodd-Frank Act, its potential success through the creation of enticing incentives and significant retaliatory protections suggests that corporations must remodel their compliance programs to ensure employees utilize internal reporting mechanisms. Under the Sarbanes-Oxley Act, an effective compliance and ethics program concerns five essential issues: (1) an environment encouraging an honest and ethical conduct; (2) accurate and timely disclosures in reports; (3) the corporation's compliance with laws; (4) the corporation's internal reporting system, capable of receiving information about possible reporting or compliance issues; and (5) holding employees accountable for complying with the corporation's code of ethics. While the SEC suggests a model "Code of Ethics," it does not entice employees to use internal reporting mechanisms when they can receive a large monetary award for informing the SEC.

Further, corporations must consider the amended Sentencing Guidelines to determine what courts will review when determining the culpability of the corporation in mitigating or increasing punishment, such as: "(i) the involvement in or tolerance of criminal activity; (ii) the prior history of the organization; (iii) the violation of an order; and (iv) the obstruction of justice." The Sentencing Guidelines also express two specific factors that can mitigate the ultimate punishment of an organization: "(i) the existence of an effective compliance and ethics program; and (ii) self-reporting, cooperation, or acceptance of responsibility."

[...]

Motivating Incentives

Corporations can motivate employees to report internally by creating a comfortable environment for internal whistleblowing that inspires loyalty and rewards trust.

Through an effective training program, management can educate employees on the standards and procedures required for compliance. An employee should know that honesty and ethical conduct is important to the corporation. If the employer has a strong ethical environment, the employee may feel that external reporting is disloyal. Corporations should reward the American psyche by acknowledging the whistleblower's loyalty to the corporation.

Most importantly, corporations can discourage loyal employees from reporting externally by communicating with employees and addressing complaints promptly. The corporation must assure the whistleblower that the allegation is taken seriously, because a whistleblower who knows that the corporation is pursuing a fair investigation will trust the compliance process and will not report externally before the conclusion of the internal investigation. However, when a hotline does not record names and contact numbers, communicating with the employee is difficult; some compliance programs assign the whistleblower a number and encourage the whistleblower to call back for an update in fourteen days. This is beneficial to both the employee and the employer, as the whistleblower can stay informed and the employer can continue to speak with the employee regarding his allegation of fraud.

[…]

Conclusion

Whistleblower incentives are not a novel concept in the United States; yet, the psychological conflict that inundates a potential employee with no particular legal knowledge is overwhelming. If a whistleblower chooses to disregard his allegiance to the corporation, he faces the difficulty of interpreting the Dodd-Frank Act and deciding whether he qualifies for an award. Yet based on past whistleblower incentives, the Dodd-Frank Act may be an intense motivator for external whistleblowing. However, there have been no Dodd-Frank Act whistleblower awards and employees are left with little guidance as to the scope and requirements of the act. Further, the employee must consider the risk associated with disclosing her identity to the SEC and having fewer protections than corporate anonymous compliance programs. These whistleblower obstacles should not make a corporation complacent because the Dodd-Frank Act has sufficient benefits and safeguards to entice an employee to use its provisions—particularly if the employee is not comfortable with the internal corporate compliance program.

Corporations can make internal whistleblowing a simple process by implementing straightforward procedures, ensuring confidentiality, rewarding loyalty, and providing an independent, uncorrupted compliance officer. This Comment suggests that even with the lack of funding, the SEC's power to award monetary incentives may successfully entice employees to externally blow the whistle; however, these incentives can be overcome by promoting an effective compliance program with greater retaliation provisions. A corporation with a good compliance program can reduce the number of external whistleblowers, increase the use of internal reporting mechanisms, and capitalize on sentencing benefits by self-reporting securities law violations.

Revealing Wrongdoing Has Strengthened Our Institutions

Gerald G. Moy

Gerald G. Moy is an affiliate of Food Safety Consultants International, which is based in Switzerland. He has published dozens of articles on public health and food industries worldwide.

From the earliest civilizations, those seeking economic gain have at times subjected the food supply to unsafe, illegal, and unethical practices. While only a small number are thought to be involved, perpetrators of such practices can include anyone who has access to the food supply chain from producers to retailers. The current size and complexity of the international agri-food network makes the food supply chain more vulnerable to such unscrupulous practices. In some cases, organized crime is involved in a food business as part of a larger criminal enterprise. If discovered, companies that undertake such practices may face expensive recalls, criminal penalties, liabilities, and possible bankruptcy. Such practices can also result in significant economic losses for the food industry as a whole. Ethical companies may lose market share to unethical competitors who are able to sell their products at lower prices. If a particular food is implicated as unsafe or fraudulent, consumers may lose confidence in the safety of all brands of that food. This can cause losses for food businesses that are honest and law abiding. Other losses are the general erosion of confidence in the safety and integrity of the food supply and in good governance by responsible authorities. While food fraud harms the consumer economically, potential risks to health and nutrition are major concerns.

"The role of whistleblowers in protecting the safety and integrity of the food supply," by Gerald G. Moy, Springer Nature Limited, May 8, 2018. https://www.nature.com/articles/s41538-018-0017-5. Licensed Under CC BY-ND 4.0.

In Medieval Europe, trade guilds established ethical codes maintained largely by peer pressure to address this problem. In modern times, the food industry has continued to promote the safety and integrity of the food supply through cooperative programs. For example, the Global Food Safety Initiative (GFSI) is a collaborative effort among the world's leading food safety experts from manufacturing, retail, and food service companies to provide continuous improvement in food safety management systems to ensure confidence in the delivery of safe food to consumers. The GFSI benchmarks food safety standards for manufacturers as well as safety assurance standards for farms.

While the food industry has primary responsibility for the safety and integrity of the foods they produce, countries have enacted laws governing food to promote a safe and honestly presented food supply. Enforcement of these laws is now universally considered to be an essential public health function of any government. The media also plays a critical role by informing the public of unsafe and fraudulent food products. They also help to mobilized consumer demand for better food safety protections. In the early part of the last century, the first food safety law in the United States was precipitated by an investigative journalist who exposed the unsanitary conditions in the Chicago stockyards.

Challenges of the Globalized Food Supply Chain

Today, the food sector is one of the largest and most important areas of economic productivity in almost every country. In 2016, the world food and agriculture market was worth about US$ 8 trillion and in 2015 global trade in food exceeded US$ 1.3 trillion. Within this complex international network, food businesses must rely on all parties meeting their responsibilities to provide safe and honestly presented products. However, long food supply chains that cross multiple jurisdictions are vulnerable to fraud, for example, the horsemeat scandal in Europe. While food fraud is mostly an economic issue, the temptation to illegally cut corners can inadvertently turn into a food safety crisis. The 2008 melamine incident in China is a case in point where melamine was added to watered-down raw milk to fool quality tests. When children and infants consumed the adulterated milk and infant formula made from the milk, about 300,000 of them experienced adverse kidney and urinary tract effects, such as kidney stones, including six reported deaths. This was one of the biggest food fraud cases to every be uncovered in which tainted products were exported to over 40 countries.

The importance of whistleblowers in protecting the safety and integrity of the food supply is illustrated by a major salmonella outbreak that occurred in the USA in 2008. Kenneth Kendrick was the assistance plant manager at a Texas peanut processing plant when he observed serious hygienic problems and improper quality control practices that were being perpetrated by the management of the now-defunct Peanut Corporation of America. Well before the outbreak occurred, he attempted to disclose this to state government and the food industry, but no one appeared interested. When the outbreak of salmonellosis caused by contaminated peanuts finally occurred, thousands of people were made ill, including nine reported fatalities. As the peanuts were used extensively in a variety of finished products, a massive recall ensued with the total cost to the food industry estimated to be over US$1 billion. The company went out of business and several company officials were sentence to prison for their actions. In response to this and other incidents, whistleblower protections in the USA were incorporated into the Food Safety Modernization Act (FSMA) of 2011.

A whistleblower's perspective is unique in that she or he is on the job every day and is often more knowledgeable about an operation and a product than anyone else. Responsible management needs internal whistleblowers to provide critical information from the "shop floor" to prevent costly mistakes that can lead to severe financial loss and harm to the public. Management should proactively seek to address safety problems as part of its public health posture, which is required by most modern food safety legislation. This also contributes to food defense, which is growing concern in some countries. Moreover, a robust internal whistleblowing system is simply a prudent business practice that facilitates communication. For example, an effective internal whistleblowing system between engineers and management could have prevented the Challenger disaster.

[...]

Whistleblowing Legislation Around the World
[...]

North America
In the United States, the 2011 FSMA offers comprehensive protections to whistleblowers who have provided information relating to any violation of the food safety and fraud regulations of the US Food, Drug and Cosmetic Act to their employer, the Federal Government, or the attorney general of a state. Also covered are whistleblowers who have testified, assisted, or participated in a proceeding concerning a violation of FSMA and its regulations; and those that objected to or refused to participate in any activity that he or she reasonably believed to be in violation of the food regulations. Retaliation against an employee for whistleblowing is specifically prohibited, including protection against firing or reassigning, reducing pay or overtime, blacklisting or failing to hire, demoting or denying promotions, denying benefits, intimidating or making threats, and disciplining. In addition, a law dating from the US Civil War in the 1860s provides that whistleblowers, including those in the food sector, who reveal that false claims or fraud were made against the Federal Government, are entitled to monetary rewards. From 2011 to the end of 2016, 280 whistleblower complaints have been filed under FSMA. Of these, 62 cases were resolved to the satisfaction of the employee and another 50 cases are still under investigation. Two other cases resulted in prosecutions. About 165 other cases were withdrawn or dismissed, mainly because the whistleblower had failed to provide additional information.

[...]

Impediments to Whistleblowing

The first impediment may be cultural because in many countries, some people associate whistleblowers with certain negative stereotypes, such as those who ingratiate themselves with authority figures. Some persons may also believe that whistleblowers are disgruntled employees with psychological problems. Others may view whistleblower as having illegally obtained their information, such as hackers who have stolen information through the internet. At times, information may relate to national security, in which case whistleblowers may be cast as disloyal. In some cases, whistleblowers have been motivated by monetary rewards. Whistleblowers might also make their colleagues uncomfortable because many of them have stayed silent although they were aware of the wrongdoing. This all may lead to the isolation and shunning of whistleblowers, which serves to dissuade other potential whistleblowers. In reality, whistleblowers often pay a high price for their reporting or disclosures.

A second impediment is the low socio-economic status of many food industry workers that makes them vulnerable to retaliation. Many are minimum-wage employees that may have little incentive to report illegal or unethical practices that they might observe. Often they may not be aware of company policies and mechanisms for internal reporting and of the legal protections that are in place to prevent retribution. The fact that some of the biggest food fraud scandals were not reported by whistleblowers indicates that whistleblowing, while good in concept, may not be wholly reliable in practice.

The third impediment is that internal reporting systems of many companies may be flawed or even non-existent. Some companies may have even suppressed the whistleblower's information and have subjected whistleblower to retaliation. In countries with no legal protections, a whistleblower may be forced to deal with a company which often have significant legal resources. Other businesses may have established internal whistleblowing policies and procedures, but their implementation may have been ad hoc and subject to conflicts of interest. For example, a whistleblower may be required to report to her or his immediate supervisor who may be the cause of the problem in the first place. Finally, some managers may operate in the negative mode—that is, they use punishment instead of reward to motivate their employees. Under such conditions, personnel may be discouraged from internal whistleblowing.

The fourth impediment resides in governments. While some progress is being made, many countries do not have any protections for whistleblowers and most do not specifically address whistleblowers in the private sector. In a critical industry such as food, this may lead managers to limit their internal whistleblowing efforts. Another factor is that government enforcement priorities are usually based on health significance and few resources are available for consumer fraud issues. Consequently, some whistleblower tips involving fraud may not be pursued. If nothing is done with the information provided, potential whistleblowers may become reluctant to inform outside authorities of problems. Even when legislation exists, some governments may not provide effective protection for qualified whistleblowers from retaliation by their employers. Some governments have even prosecuted whistleblowers for disclosing protected or confidential information in spite of the illegal activities that were revealed.

[...]

Despite Personal Risk, Whistleblowing Is Essential to Society

Transparency International

Over the last twenty-five years, the Transparency International non-governmental organization has worked with governments, businesses, and citizens to address corruption and other misuses of power. It is based in Berlin, Germany.

Whistleblowing is increasingly recognised as an important tool in the prevention and detection of corruption and other malpractice. By disclosing wrongdoing in an organisation, whistleblowers can avert harm, protect human rights, help to save lives and safeguard the rule of law. The clandestine nature of corrupt behaviour means that it may never come to light unless cases are reported by people who discover them in the course of their work. But reporting can come at a high price: whistleblowers often expose themselves to great personal risks in order to protect the public interest. As a result of speaking out, they may lose their jobs, dampen their career prospects, and even put their own lives at risk. To provide a safe alternative to silence, TI recommends policy and legal measures to provide:

- Effective legal protection of whistleblowers against retaliation with full compensation in case of reprisals;
- Adequate mechanisms in public, private and not-for-profit organisations to ensure that disclosures are properly handled and thoroughly investigated;
- Public research, data collection, information and training to inform about the public benefit of whistleblowing.

What Is Whistleblowing?

Whistleblowing is the disclosure of information about perceived wrongdoing in an organisation, or the risk thereof, to individuals or entities believed to be able to effect action. The ultimate goal of whistleblowing is to protect the public interest. It achieves this by informing people or organisations that are in a position to prevent harm, to investigate or to take action against those responsible for wrongdoing. Prominent whistleblowers have revealed the cover-up of SARS and other dangerous diseases and helped to avoid environmental and health hazards in the United States and elsewhere.

Data shows that occurrences of fraud in companies often come to light thanks to whistleblowers who have been found in some studies to detect internal problems more frequently than any other actor, including regulators, auditors and the media.

Protecting one's right to come forth with wrongdoings is closely related to protecting one's freedom of expression and conscience. It also is based on the principles of transparency and accountability.

The Role of Whistleblowing in the Fight Against Corruption

Corruption is a notoriously secretive activity and it is usually only those engaged in corrupt deals or those who work with them that are aware of it. Insiders are among the few people who are able to report cases of corruption (past or ongoing) and identify the risk of future wrongdoing. By helping to detect corruption cases, whistleblowers play a critical role in converting a vicious cycle of secrecy into a virtuous cycle. Detection of corruption is a pre-condition to initiate related investigations and prosecution. However, only if corruption cases are effectively prosecuted can a culture of corruption change.

Major bribery and corruption scandals demonstrate the damage done by the failure to report wrongdoing as soon as it is discovered. Yet indifference, fear of reprisal, and misplaced loyalty as well as an overall culture of silence often deter potential witnesses and whistleblowers from speaking out.

The Relevance of Appropriate Whistleblowing Legislation

Appropriate whistleblowing legislation and the means to enforce it are necessary to support a culture of compliance and integrity. Several international conventions recognise whistleblowing as an effective tool for fighting corruption, fraud and mismanagement, and commit the signatory countries to implement appropriate legislation. However, existing legal provisions are fragmented and weakly enforced in most jurisdictions. Only in rare cases do they provide sufficient protection for whistleblowers.

[…]

Recommendations

Together with international experts, Transparency International has produced a set of guiding principles for drafting whistleblowing legislation. These principles provide a comprehensive framework for related laws, building on international best practice. Below are the recommendations derived from these principles.

A Single, Comprehensive Legal Framework Is Most Effective

To ensure a safe alternative to silence for whistleblowers, the legal framework should be clear, comprehensive and easy to use for protecting the whistleblower. Ideally, a single legislative framework should be in place, but provisions in different bills can fulfil the same purpose if they do not leave loopholes or become too complicated. In all cases, the legislation should cover the public, private, and not-for-profit sectors and provide for reliable reporting channels to communicate concerns. Legislation should include a broad range of issues, from criminal offences to the potential harm that wrongdoing can cause, such as to the health and safety of citizens and the environment. Whistleblowing legislation should provide that organisations in the public and private sector establish, maintain, and routinely publicise appropriate mechanisms for internal reporting.

Safety Should Be Ensured for Whistleblowers

Both public and private employees and those outside the traditional employee-employer relationship (e.g. consultants, temporary workers, trainees, etc.) should be protected from reprisal for honestly reporting concerns. Protection should also be extended to those attempting to report or corroborating reports and include a right to refuse participation in wrongdoings. Any individuals closely associated with the whistleblower, such as family members, should be covered as well. In case of retaliation against the whistleblower, the burden of proof to show that this discrimination is not related should lie with the employer. These protections should be guaranteed by access to normal court procedures.

Whistleblowers should be protected against any damages suffered as a consequence of their disclosure. They should receive some kind of professional or social recognition for having prevented excessive harm to the organisation or society. Such a system, potentially including financial rewards, should be carefully designed, taking the particular national and legal contexts into account.

Internal and External Reporting Should Be Protected

Where possible, reports or concerns should first be raised internally and to the appropriate body set up by the organisation with assurances that whistleblower confidentiality is clearly established. This allows organisations time and space to investigate the nature and substance of a report without unfairly exposing the subject of a report or the organisation to unfounded allegations.

In many instances, however, initially reporting internally might not be a possibility. Whistleblowers may fear retaliation for filing an internal report, the report may not be followed up internally for various reasons (e.g. where malpractices are institutionalised or where managers are concerned about the negative impact on the image of the institution or on themselves), or the public interest may be best served by immediately filing the report externally to the authorities or other agencies. Whistleblowers should have a safe option to report externally to the regulator, enforcement authorities or to other competent oversight bodies. This is particularly important in cases where there is an immediate risk to the health and safety of people. As a last resort, disclosures to the media should also be protected.

The British Public Interest Disclosure Act (PIDA), for instance, takes different factors and consequences of whistleblowing for people and organisations into account. It is an example of a model that allows for internal and external reporting, establishing three levels of disclosure

Enforcement Is Essential

While the existence of a legal framework is a pre-condition for whistleblower protection, it is not sufficient. Legislation needs to be effectively enforced and should be as sound and consistent as possible. To ensure the proper implementation of legal provisions, an independent public body with sufficient autonomy should be set up or designated to oversee the functioning of the law and to receive and investigate complaints. Enforcement should include consultations with key stakeholders like trade unions, business associations and civil society actors so that whistleblowing policies can be agreed upon and put into effect.

The Need for Effective Follow-Up Mechanisms in Organisations

To realise the potential of whistleblowing legislation, the legal framework should be complemented with effective follow-up mechanisms in organisations. There also must be a willingness in organisations (whether a public institution, private company or not-for-profit) to provide sufficient resources, to investigate cases through independent bodies, to implement necessary changes and to hold those responsible for wrongdoing to account.

In recognition of the potential of whistleblowing for effective risk management in organisations, a number of related provisions and guidelines have been developed. The Sarbanes-Oxley Act, a law in the US which sets financial reporting standards for public companies, mandates whistleblower protection mechanisms for public companies registered in the country The International Chamber of Commerce also has adopted voluntary guidelines and the British Standards Institute has developed a code which establishes best practice for whistleblowing in organisations.

[...]

The Financial Gains from Whistleblowing in the US

The US False Claims Act is considered one of the strongest and most effective whistleblowing laws in the world. It contains *qui tam* provisions, a mechanism that allows citizens with evidence of fraud against government contracts to sue, on behalf of the government, in order to recover the stolen funds.

In compensation for the risk and effort of filing a *qui tam* case, the whistleblower may be awarded a portion of the funds recovered, typically between 15 and 25 per cent.

According to the US Department of Justice Civil Fraud Division, the United States has recovered more than US$ 21 billion since 1986 thanks to the False Claims Act. Studies estimate the fraud deterred by the *qui tam* provisions runs into the hundreds of billions of dollars.

The Demand for a Shift in Culture

The importance of whistleblowing in the detection and prevention of wrongdoing is still generally under-valued. It is an inexpensive risk management tool with particular benefits for emerging democracies with less established oversight mechanisms. Whistleblowing is also a tool to sound the alarm at early stages, potentially even before any damage has been caused. Nevertheless, whistleblowers are often perceived as disloyal, rather than as champions of the public interest. In many countries they are viewed as untrustworthy, and sometimes even as spies or traitors.

Recommendations

Public Support Is Needed to Promote Whistleblowing

To change this perception, whistleblowing needs to be promoted as an effective tool for stopping corruption and serving the public interest. Governments should lend their support to public information campaigns as well as initiatives to promote whistleblowing that are carried out by professional groups, Ombudspersons, industry, media, trade unions and other civil society organisations. Whistleblowers should not only be protected by public authorities, but also honoured and actively supported.

Data on the Public Benefit of Whistleblowing Should Be Collected and Published

Data from the United States show the relevance of whistleblowing for the recovery of public revenues. Yet on a global scale there is little data available on the number of cases reported, the effectiveness of reporting channels and the financial benefits due to whistleblowing. This lack of data could be addressed by making more court and tribunal decisions public and by standardising whistleblowing procedures across the public sector. Given the central role of whistleblowing in detecting and preventing wrongdoing, gathering reliable statistics will greatly help decision-makers and the public to measure progress in uncovering corruption.

A Proper Societal and Legal Environment Is Needed

A legislative environment, ensuring freedom of expression, access to information and the existence of an independent media are critical to enable a culture of whistleblowing. Protection of journalists' sources should include information provided by whistleblowers, even if journalists might base their reports at times on erroneous information given in good faith. The growing relevance of internet tools provides whistleblowers with new channels for reporting and thereby creates a global platform which increasingly can help ensure that whistleblowing becomes and remains an important issue in the public debate.

Veteran Case Studies Reveal the Necessity of Whistleblowing

Eric Westervelt

Westervelt has been an NPR correspondent since 2003. He covers stories in the Middle East and in the United States and focuses on warfare, law enforcement, and political unrest.

Alan Hyde is a veteran of the US Marine Corps and the Central Alabama Veterans Health Care System. He served in Operation Desert Storm, where he suffered an in-service leg injury. But it's his time with the Central Alabama VA, he says, that has left him more rattled, frustrated and angry.

"It's a toxic environment there," Hyde says. "And I feel sorry for the veterans."

Hyde is both a patient and a former employee at the Central Alabama Veterans Health Care System in Montgomery. He supervised employees who took vets for treatment outside the VA. Hyde was fired after six months for unspecified misconduct. He is among dozens of people who say they faced vicious retaliation when they tried to improve conditions there or hold managers accountable.

More than 30 current and former VA employees spoke to NPR. They include doctors, nurses and administrators — many of them veterans themselves. All describe an entrenched management culture that uses fear and intimidation to prevent potential whistleblowers from talking.

"If you say anything about patient care and the problems, you're quickly labeled a troublemaker and attacked by a clique that just promotes itself. Your life becomes hell," one longtime employee at the Central Alabama Veterans Health Care System, or CAVHCS, told NPR. Like many we interviewed there, she requested anonymity out of fear for her job.

The problems are especially acute at hospital complexes in Montgomery and Tuskegee, Ala., which are part of a regional network known as VA Southeast Network VISN 7. The Department of Veterans Affairs divides veterans' health care into 21 geographic regions called VISNs.

Workers say the retaliatory tactics run the gamut from sophomoric (a shift manager pouring salt into a subordinate's coffee cup) to hard-to-fathom (isolation rooms used as psychological coercion) and more.

"There's no accountability," Hyde says. "And it's gonna be a never-ending cycle here until someone steps in and starts cleaning house from the top and putting people in who care about the veterans."

But neither those charged with federal oversight nor the VA itself has taken those steps, months or even years after the first complaints were reported.

[...]

Why are conditions so bad in Central Alabama? Watchdog groups and affected workers believe it's a combination of weak, inconsistent enforcement of whistleblower protection laws, a senior managerial culture that practices and condones bullying, and a VA system that too often sends whistleblower grievances right back to regional managers who are often part of the original complaints.

The scope of the retaliation and sheer number of retaliation complaints in VISN 7 and across the agency raise questions about whether the VA can adequately police itself and embrace whistleblowers as President Trump and the VA have vowed to do.

Stealing Food from Vets

"I hadn't been there [Central Alabama] two weeks when an employee came in to tell me about illegal activities in the kitchen, and he stopped right there and he said, 'But if you're not going to do anything about it, I'm going to keep my mouth shut, otherwise I become the target,'" says retired US Army Col. Cynthia Chavez.

Chavez has some 50 years of combined Army active duty, Reserve and VA service. She has consistent outstanding or exceptional performance reviews across both institutions.

In June 2014, she was hired to lead Nutrition and Food Services for Central Alabama's VA. She soon found that both the Montgomery and Tuskegee hospital kitchens — especially Tuskegee's — had serious, systemic problems.

Some employees, she says, routinely came in late, left early or didn't show up at all. One, she says, would openly drink on the job. That employee once told a veteran in a PTSD program, " 'I'll give you the bullet to put in the gun to shoot yourself,' " she says.

Remarkably, that wasn't the worst of it.

Chavez was told that a longtime employee was allegedly running a side catering business out of the VA kitchen in Tuskegee.

"She was using government employees, government food, on government time, for her catering business," Chavez says. "She was selling it [food] through her catering business" to area companies and churches. "And so when I did my due diligence, sure enough, she couldn't answer questions about how she'd catered this event and yet she was on duty."

One Valentine's Day, for example, a case of steaks and cheesecakes meant for a special hospital meal for vets went missing. Several co-workers told Chavez the thievery had been going on for years.

Chavez was shocked and moved quickly to investigate and temporarily suspend the employee, emails and documents show. She also imposed stronger discipline and order on a hospital kitchen she says "was like the Wild West. They [employees] did what they wanted to." All the food in the kitchen is from appropriated funds meant only for veterans in hospital treatment. "Myself, as a 30-year veteran, I couldn't even eat there."

Soon after, Chavez got the first of many anonymous-threat letters slipped under her Tuskegee office door. "This isn't the Army, where you had connections. This is the VA and we will get you," one letter said.

But Chavez says that the anonymous-threat letters were only slightly more menacing than what she soon got from her boss and the local union leaders.

Following an almost classic whistleblower retaliation script, instead of support, Chavez was soon investigated for "abuse of authority" and "creating a hostile work environment."

The union, Tuskegee AFGE Local 110, quickly announced it had taken a vote of "no confidence" in Chavez.

And her top boss, a career VA employee named Leslie Wiggins, soon told her in no uncertain terms to back off.

In fact, Wiggins then took charge of all discipline and oversight of the VA's troubled hospital kitchen. She also stripped Chavez of all the authority and oversight she had been hired to impose on the department. The reason given, emails and documents show, was Chavez's "inappropriate disciplinary actions" against the food service staff.

When a local union official complained that Chavez was issuing what he called "unsubstantiated" AWOLs, or absent without leave sanctions, Wiggins — then serving as acting director of CAVHCS as well as head of VISN 7 — emailed Chavez: "This is a very disturbing email" about what "may be a problem practice" of issuing AWOLs. "So until further notice," Wiggins wrote, "there are to be NO AWOL's issued until I review them."

"I am trying to hold employees accountable and all I get is pushback through anonymous letters," Chavez says. "And even when HR was saying, 'No, she's justified in what she's trying to do,' they would not let me take any discipline against anything that the employees were doing."

She notified federal offices that she was the target of whistleblower retaliation. Nothing, so far, has come of it.

Chavez eventually went out on medical leave to care for her cancer-stricken husband.

This past January, Chavez's boss and Central Alabama's director, Linda Boyle, emailed her: "The decision has been made to terminate you effective January, 30, 2018."

Chavez's request to be allowed to retire at the end of March and to use her remaining sick leave to help her husband was denied. She reluctantly retired.

Despite several Freedom of Information Act requests, Chavez has never seen details of the charges brought against her in what's known as an Administrative Investigation Board (AIB).

The woman who was allegedly stealing food from veterans for years through her side catering business? She was allowed to retire with full benefits. There's no indication she was ever disciplined by the VA or the local union.

Neither Wiggins nor Boyle would comment on Chavez's case or the wider pattern of retaliation.

[…]

One Whistleblower Wins

VISN 7's director Leslie Wiggins, in fact, has had numerous whistleblower retaliation complaints filed against her, including one by an employee in her immediate office in Atlanta. The federal Office of Special Counsel ruled against Wiggins and her office in a case that, as the Atlanta Journal-Constitution put it, showed that the Atlanta VA seemed more preoccupied with halting bad press coverage than stopping a series of veteran suicides in the Atlanta area.

Retired Army Sgt. Maj. Greg Kendall, a 30-year veteran with tours in Iraq and Afghanistan, took a job as a public affairs officer (PAO) in the Atlanta VA after his military service. Kendall says he raised concerns about spending tens of thousands of taxpayer dollars promoting a local charity gala that senior VA employees planned to attend. At the time, the Atlanta office was under fire for underfunding and understaffing veteran mental health services, including suicide prevention efforts.

"The leadership was not interested in my concerns and basically told me to mind my own business," Kendall says.

When the charity story went public, the Atlanta management quickly gave him a bad evaluation, placed him on a performance improvement plan, and, following the pattern, isolated him in a small, shabby, vacant patient room while he was "investigated."

"The entire leadership team knew that I was in that patient room for almost a year that could have been used for veteran care," Kendall says, but "they were more concerned about retaliation than taking care of veterans."

Kendall fought back, filing for whistleblower protection. The federal Office of Special Counsel (OSC) investigated and ruled in Kendall's favor, saying he had been targeted and punished for speaking up.

"Mr. Kendall did the right thing by raising concerns about an inappropriate expenditure of taxpayer dollars, but the Atlanta VA failed to heed his warnings and instead targeted Mr. Kendall," the Special Counsel's Carolyn Lerner wrote in the OSC ruling. Lerner added that "the VA must continue working to make its culture more welcoming to whistleblowers in all of its facilities."

Kendall says he blew the whistle after thinking about the vets he served with in Iraq and Afghanistan.

"They depend on the VA," he said. "So the very fact that we (Atlanta VA) have been cited for mismanagement that led to suicides told me that we needed to do something to make sure that that didn't happen again."

His case is one of the only whistleblower cases to succeed against VISN 7 leadership.

Can the VA Police Itself?

Nearly a year ago, the VA reorganized the unit responsible for protecting workers who call out wrongdoing, waste, fraud and abuse.

In that 11-month period, the new Office of Accountability and Whistleblower Protection (OAWP) has received 120 whistleblower complaints from VISN 7: the most complaints of retaliation per veteran served of the department's 21 VISNs.

Only VISN 22 (Southern California, Arizona and New Mexico) and VISN 8 (Florida, Puerto Rico and the US Virgin Islands) had similar numbers, but both serve a larger number of veterans. VISN 8, for example, had about 1.5 times as many completed veteran appointments in 2017, according to the VA's own patient access data.

Of those 120 complaints against VISN 7, 79 were determined to be of "reasonable belief" and 51 investigations were opened.

Yet only 11 of those 51 are currently under investigation by OAWP. The other 40 were sent back to VISN 7 or district level for investigation.

It's exactly that investigatory boomerang, critics say, that highlights why the VA is so ineffectual at policing whistleblower retaliation.

For example, emails from Walsh, the HR executive, show that during her last contact with OAWP, the office told her that her case was under investigation. But Walsh hasn't heard from OAWP in more than eight months.

"No calls, no emails, no texts, nothing. It's like we don't exist," she says.

VA spokeswoman Ashleigh Barry said the OAWP would not comment on active investigations or allegations of worker retaliation at VISN 7, but said the department takes all allegations seriously.

The Accountability and Whistleblower Protection Act expanded the authority and support for the OAWP, the VA's office that now shares the bill's name.

But a year later, there's skepticism the OAWP is living up to its name.

"We've got a very sick organization. The important thing (for the VA) is to squelch the whistleblowers to speak. You know, it's like shoot the messenger because it's not the message we want to hear," says VA whistleblower Sheila Meuse, who has 30-plus years of federal service—almost all of it at VA facilities across the country.

Meuse rose from a clinician to, in 2014, serving briefly as the third in command at Central Alabama. "I always had either outstanding or exceptional ratings," she says. "I can't remember any one rating ever that was below exceptional in my career history."

Just four months into her new job in Alabama, Meuse and her direct boss, Richard Tremaine, exposed unethical practices—part of that wait-times scandal in 2014 that played out in multiple VA hospitals across the country.

[...]

In the Medical Field, Corruption Is Usually Systemic

Jeanne Lenzer

Jeanne Lenzer investigates fraud within the medical community as a freelance journalist.

A year ago, I received an E-mail from a research scientist at a major pharmaceutical company. The scientist had read my articles on whistleblowers who had raised concerns about the undue influence of the pharmaceutical industry on American medicine. My industry source had information for me about drug company practices, but—out of fear of career ruin—would only talk on the condition that I would conceal the scientist's identity.

For the next year or so, I had repeated contacts with the scientist. As I listened to this researcher—and to the other medical whistleblowers that I continued to interview—it occurred to me that each whistleblower was like the proverbial blind man with a hand on the elephant. Each could describe one piece of the puzzle, but the full picture could only emerge by bringing these whistleblowers together.

With an eye to focusing on the systemic problems that have allowed American medicine to be unduly influenced by industry, on May 15, 2005, I brought together five whistleblowers in Washington, D. C. I asked them each to tell their story and to suggest ways to restore objectivity to medicine and medical research.

The Whistleblowers

Four whistleblowers attended in person, and the anonymous industry scientist participated via speakerphone. The

"What Can We Learn from Medical Whistleblowers?" by Jeanne Lenzer, Public Library of Science (PLOS), May 27, 2005. https://www.ncbi.nlm.nih.gov/pmc/articles/PMC1140678/. Licensed Under CC BY-ND 4.0.

whistleblowers came from an extraordinary variety of different professional backgrounds.

David Graham: This Food and Drug Administration (FDA) safety officer raised concerns about the cardiovascular side effects of rofecoxib (Vioxx) and other Cox-2 inhibitors. He testified at a United States Senate Finance Committee hearing on rofexocib, the FDA, and Merck. Graham attended the roundtable in his own personal capacity and was not representing the FDA.

Allen Jones: This investigator at the Pennsylvania Office of the Inspector General led an investigation into an off-the-books account, funded in part by drug companies, from which payments were made to state employees to develop a medication treatment algorithm. He filed a civil rights lawsuit against the Pennsylvania Office of the Inspector General to protect his right to publicly discuss his findings, and was later fired from his job for talking to the press.

Stefan Kruszewski: This Harvard-trained psychiatrist was hired by the Bureau of Program Integrity in the Pennsylvania Department of Public Welfare to oversee the state's mental health and substance misuse programs. He filed a law suit in a federal court in the Middle District of Pennsylvania, charging that he was fired after uncovering widespread abuse and fraud in the bureau.

Kathleen Slattery-Moschkau: This former drug representative left the pharmaceutical industry after witnessing marketing practices that she found disturbing. She wrote and directed the movie *Side Effects*, a fictionalized account of her experiences.

The anonymous research scientist: This is an industry insider who said to me, ahead of the roundtable, that the culture of secrecy at drug companies too often results in claims that are closer to "propaganda" than science.

Lessons Learned from the Roundtable
Ties Between Drug Regulators and Industry May Influence New Drug Approval

David Graham described the frustrations he had felt in his almost 20 years of experience as an FDA drug safety officer. Although he was instrumental, he said, in getting ten drugs off the market because of safety concerns, his experience was like a salmon swimming upstream—"a single individual…against the tide." The tide, he said, "is an entire institution whose mission is to approve drugs and make industry happy."

The FDA, said Graham, is in a "collaborative relationship" with industry. The FDA gets money from drug companies through the Prescription Drug User Fee Act of 1992 (see http://www.fda.gov/cber/pdufa.htm) "to approve new drugs and approve them more quickly." The mindset at the FDA, he said, is that "we will find a reason to approve a drug no matter how small the indication for the drug." Graham explained that a senior official at the FDA had told him: "industry is our client."

When the FDA knows there is a serious problem with a new drug, he said, the FDA deals with this by saying, "well, we'll handle it in labeling" even though, said Graham, "FDA knows labeling doesn't work."

"There is no independent voice for drug safety in the United States," he said. The upper-level managers in the FDA's Office of Drug Safety are appointed from the FDA's Office of New Drugs, which approves new medicines. This makes the Office of Drug Safety "captive," he said, to the Office of New Drugs.

The anonymous scientist said that in order to speed up drug approval, companies "don't measure things like whether we are really curing the disease, or prolonging life, or preventing hospitalization, or whether a patient is truly more functional. Oftentimes, we're measuring intermediate, lesser things, markers, predictors—we *hope*—of these clinical endpoints, but they may or may not be accurate."

And the FDA, said the scientist, requires just two positive studies to grant approval to a new drug, but there is no limitation on how many negative studies can be done before one or two positive studies are produced. This can lead to approval of a drug even when most studies are negative or show no effect.

Both Graham and the anonymous scientist suggested putting an end to the Prescription Drug User Fee Act, and Graham argued that there needs to be independent authority for those in charge of drug safety. They indicated that two bills in Congress, introduced by Senator Grassley and by Congressman Hinchey, at least partly address these concerns.

"The pharma–FDA complex has to be dismantled," said Graham, "and the American people have to insist on that, otherwise we're going to have disasters like Vioxx that happen in the future."

The Race to Approve New Drugs Without Proper Safety Testing May Be Compromising the Public's Health

"Drug companies assiduously avoid acquiring information about side effects," said the industry scientist. "Drug companies will not conduct safety studies unless they have to—meaning basically that they're required by a regulator—and that rarely happens." High-risk patients who might have a bad reaction to a drug, said the scientist, "are excluded from studies deliberately, even though, when the drug is approved, these patients will be targeted for sales." When a safety study is proposed within the industry, said the scientist, "a typical response will be that if we conducted a study to find out if there was a safety problem, people would learn about it and think we *had* a problem [which] would destroy the image of safety that has been so carefully constructed."

Studies are too small and are conducted over too brief a period to properly assess safety: "The largest studies—the phase three studies, [which] might be several thousand people—last for a few months. If drugs kill one in several thousand per year, this would be a public health catastrophe. A blockbuster drug with that kind of hazard associated with it could be associated with tens of thousands of deaths a year, and it would never be detected in studies of the kind that we routinely submit and are the basis for approval." These drugs, said the scientist, and these kinds of risks, are "essentially out there now, unlabeled, unnoticed, all beneath the radar."

The scientist said that, "to ensure that safety problems will go unnoticed, we compound the problem of conducting small studies by setting a statistical threshold for acknowledging the safety problem that is so high that you know in advance it could never be reached for any serious side effect, like myocardial infarction." This practice, said the scientist, "virtually ensures that if a bad side effect happens to show up, it's not going to reach the arbitrary level that we call statistically significant, and the company can maintain that it's just bad luck." And if a bad result does happen, "typically a company is not going to publish the study at all. If they do publish it, the bad result can be omitted as 'not statistically important.'"

The Funding of State Officials May Be Affecting Prescribing Patterns

Allen Jones described how he believed that drug companies were acting at the state level to influence the prescribing of psychiatric medications.

"I began to investigate an account into which pharmaceutical companies were paying money that was being accessed by state employees," he said. "Additionally, I found that various pharmaceutical companies were paying state employees directly— also giving them trips, perks, lavish meals, transportation, honorariums up to $2,000 for speaking in their official capacities at drug company events. They were given unrestricted educational grants that were deposited into an off-the-books account— unregistered, unmonitored, literally operated out of a drawer."

These same state officials, he said, were responsible for dictating clinical policy and writing guidelines for the treatment of patients in the state system. These officials were, he said, receiving money from companies with a stake in the guidelines. "The protocol they [the officials] were developing was called the Texas Medication Algorithm Project, TMAP, which began in Texas in the mid-90s. It outlined detailed medication guidelines for schizophrenia, depression, and bipolar disorder. It recommends almost exclusive usage of newer, patented, very expensive atypical antipsychotics, SSRIs [selective serotonin uptake inhibitors], and mood stabilizers." The Texas Medication Algorithm Project, said Jones, was based on "expert consensus" from industry-supported meetings.

Jones said that when he wanted to investigate these findings, he was shut down. "I was told pointblack, 'Look, drug companies write checks to politicians, they write checks to politicians on both sides of the aisle—back off.'" He was told, he said, to "quit being a salmon, quit swimming against a stream." He wouldn't back down from his investigation, he said, and was demoted. On November 22, 2002, he filed a civil rights lawsuit "to preserve my job and my right to speak out." His employer, he said, took him off investigative duties altogether.

Stefan Kruszewski, who has filed a law suit in a federal court in Pennsylvania, raised concerns to his seniors in the Pennsylvania Department of Public Welfare about prescribing practices in the state that he did not feel were evidence based, and said he lost his job for raising his concerns. For example, he alerted his seniors to the off-label prescribing of the anticonvulsant gabapentin (Neurontin) for mood disorders and addictive disorders.

"The pharmaceutical industry is the single most powerful lobbying group on Capitol Hill—outspending even the oil and banking industries," said Jones. "It should come as no surprise that the ties go far beyond just the mental health officials who wrote the guidelines, but extend to many of the politicians who, in the end, allowed an investigation into pharma corruption to be dropped, and the investigator—me—to be fired."

Efforts to detect and deter fraud and abuse due to these conflicts, he said, "will be likely to be undermined as long as those charged with detecting fraud and abuse, like the [Pennsylvania] Inspector General, are appointed by politicians who are themselves beholden to the drug industry. Such positions should instead be filled by career civil servants and not political appointees."

Regulatory Agencies Are Not Being Held Accountable

In comments that echoed his testimony to the US Senate Finance Committee, Graham said that, "FDA was the single greatest obstacle to doing anything effective with Vioxx. As a result, nearly 60,000 people probably died from that drug. That's as many of our soldiers that were killed in the Vietnam war [who] died as a result of Vioxx use. And FDA had the opportunity, the responsibility, to stop that and didn't. In fact, FDA allowed it to continue. In my book, FDA shares in the responsibility for those deaths and yet it's not being held accountable by Congress." Congress itself, added Graham, is deeply beholden to the drug industry since many politicians receive "often quite a bit of campaign contributions" from the industry.

Kruszewski reflected upon the problems he said he had encountered in Pennsylvania, saying that "there is no accountability in the system for oversight [agencies]." He has become "a stronger advocate than ever for a federal patient bill of rights."

Marketing Departments Can Influence Doctors' Prescribing Habits

The research scientist said that the job was attractive because of the "many excellent drugs" developed, such as drugs to treat HIV, but the scientist "also saw drugs marketed in a way that will exaggerate the benefits and conceal the risks."

Kathleen Slattery-Moschkau gave an insider's view of drug marketing practices, from her former experiences as a drug rep. She clutched her head in disbelief as she told the roundtable that doctors would come up to her with patients' charts asking her for advice on treating patients. Slattery-Moschkau, like most of the drug representatives she came to know over the years, had no science background at all.

The various techniques drug representatives were trained in to "educate doctors" eventually proved to be not just "comical" but "also scary," she said. "Whether it was hiring, training, what we were told to say about drugs and what we were told not to say," it was marketing, not science, that dominated. One of the techniques used by drug companies was to buy doctors' prescribing records so drug representatives knew "to the dime" what drugs doctors were prescribing and could tailor their marketing to them. Drug representatives developed "personality profiles" on doctors and were taught to pitch their sales to specific personality types. Representatives were compensated, she said, by "how many prescriptions we could encourage."

Both Slattery-Moschkau and the industry scientist described tensions within drug companies between marketing departments and industry scientists. "The marketing spin on things," said the scientist, "carries the day."

The Published Medical Literature Contains Many Biases
"When studies are published," said the scientist, "they are frequently written not by the trained research scientist, who might have designed and analyzed the study, but by a designated medical writer with little if any background in research, but who is trained instead to craft the findings of the study in the best possible way for the company."

The body of literature available to the public, said the scientist, "is a biased sample of what companies want people to see." The research scientist described "a culture of secrecy," which makes it hard even for industry scientists tasked with ensuring drug safety to obtain the full datasets needed to genuinely understand a drug's risk–benefit profile.

Conclusion

Whistleblowers have been compared to bees—they have just one sting to use and using it may lead to career suicide. Many of the whistleblowers at the roundtable said they had experienced retaliation from their employers for raising concerns, but all had felt obligated to speak out about practices in medicine and medical research that they believe are risking the public's health or safety. Graham said he felt "trapped by the truth" and had to act. "There are bigger issues here," said Kruszewski. "I felt right from the start [that] if I wallowed in self-pity about being fired and having my belongings piled in the gutter that I would never understand why all these things were happening. The bigger issue is that we've got people in the pharmaceutical industry and the health-care industry all acting in synchrony."

Each of these whistleblowers, in very different ways—from making a satiric film to speaking out in Congress—has shone light on how this "synchrony" may be compromising the integrity of American medicine. We should not have to rely on medical whistleblowers to alert us to these fault lines. If we are to restore objectivity to drug development, prescribing, and safety monitoring, we must be willing to examine and change all of the institutions that allow this synchrony to occur.

Fraud Is Symptomatic of Business Culture

FTI Consulting

FTI Consulting is an independent global business advisory firm that assists organizations in managing change, mitigating risk, and resolving disputes with a variety of services.

Fraud occurs every day all over the world. Some companies take an "it won't happen to us" approach; others implement controls to try to keep individuals likely to commit fraud from entering the business; and still others outsource the work of combating fraud to external auditors. These tactics and strategies are helpful but are limited. Companies must create lower risk environments for fraud. To do so, organizations first must understand their own corporate ecology — the interrelations between people and their workplace — and tailor controls to the nature of those systems.

Fraud may be as old as civilization itself. Fraudulent activity was mentioned in the Code of Hammurabi, the oldest-known surviving code of law dating to around 1772 B.C. Modern archaeologists often unearth counterfeit coins from cities long forgotten.

As long as there have been opportunities, there have been fraudsters.

Today, in an increasingly interconnected world, digital technologies that enable business to be conducted in the wink of an eye also help disguise the identities and machinations of the people conducting that business, thereby enabling fraud to become vastly more sophisticated and pervasive. Likewise, fraud's impact — on businesses, stakeholders and entire economies — has similarly magnified.

According to the Association of Certified Fraud Examiners (ACFE), fraud includes:

- Corruption (such as conflicts of interest and bribery)

"Business Fraud: Culture Is the Culprit," FTI Consulting, September 2014. Reprinted by permission.

- Asset misappropriation (through theft or illegal diversions of cash or other assets)
- Financial statement fraud (such as asset/revenue overstatement or understatement)

In its 2014 ACFE survey*, the association estimated that the typical organization loses 5 percent of its revenues every year to fraud, with an average cost per incident of $145,000 among all cases reported. The global loss in 2013 approached $3.7 trillion.

Globally, asset misappropriation represents the large majority of fraudulent activity, comprising nearly 85 percent of the total cases of occupational fraud in 2013, with a median cost of $130,000 per case. Financial statement fraud was rarer—just 9 percent of reported cases involved financial misstatements—but in these cases, the estimated loss per incident exceeded $1 million. Interestingly, two or more of these types of fraud occurred together 30 percent of the time.

According to the ACFE report, the sectors most often victimized by fraud are banking/financial, government and public administration, and manufacturing; within these sectors, the real estate, mining, and oil and gas industries reported the largest median losses. However, it is important to note that fraud differs by region. While billing (financial statement) fraud is the most common in the United States and Canada, in developing economies such as those in Latin America and Asia, corruption is rife. Therefore, companies operating in multiple jurisdictions must take regional differences into consideration when devising their anti-fraud strategies.

In other words, there is no one-size-fits-all approach to combating fraud. Nevertheless, as challenging as this might be, developing a customized approach is crucial. In the most recent ACFE survey, more than half the companies reporting fraud had not recovered any of their losses, and only 14 percent had been made whole.

Fraud Prevention: A Mug Shot

People commit fraud, but it's nearly impossible to identify a potential fraudster with any degree of confidence. The overwhelming majority of people who commit fraud are first-time offenders. Only 5 percent of fraudsters caught have had a prior fraud conviction. Therefore, no matter how diligently a background check is conducted, the likelihood that it will unmask a person who eventually will steal from the business is vanishingly small.

This is not to say that companies should neglect conducting due diligence in their hiring processes. Just like internal and external audits, screening processes are among a business' first lines of defense and should remain a part of the company's good housekeeping practices. But these practices are not as effective as commonly believed; ACFE statistics show that external auditing—while essential to good corporate governance—is the least effective type of anti-fraud control, detecting only 3 percent of frauds, compared to the 7 percent that are discovered by accident.

The implementation of internal controls is more effective, and obviously more proactive, than external ex post facto audits. These controls should include management reviews, real-time (or as close to it as feasible) data analysis of transactions, robust whistleblower programs, rigorous client and partner vetting, and a wide range of soft compliance strategies, including tipster hotlines, qualitative interviews with employees and a process for continually collecting employee feedback. Not only do these strategies help companies keep their finger on the pulse of the organization, anti-fraud policies also help deter potential fraudsters who would take advantage of a company's lack of such oversight.

Unfortunately, these anti-fraud strategies rarely are deployed in a repeatable, ongoing manner. Proactive data monitoring, for example, was used by only 35 percent of the victimized companies surveyed in the 2014 ACFE survey, even though companies that did deploy data monitoring experienced frauds that were 60 percent less costly and 50 percent shorter in duration.

Instead of working to create an environment less vulnerable and less hospitable to fraudsters and fraudulent activities, companies sometimes put undue attention on identifying individual perpetrators. This leads some businesses down the dangerous path of screening prospective employees for ill-defined desirable or undesirable personality traits and conducting employment interviews that frequently are biased and may open doors to discrimination lawsuits. This kind of personality-focused interviewing and testing (most often conducted by Human Resources (HR)) also can cause companies to miss out on top talent that might be screened out due to cultural differences but that could have been addressed easily through cultural-awareness training.

Any anti-fraud measures that take the organization's eye off its own culture—either by chasing after individuals or outsourcing the problem to third parties—will leave an environment that is wide open for providing fertile ground for fraud and fraudsters to take root and thrive.

The Ecology of Fraud

Remember: People commit fraud, and because people are social animals, their actions, in great measure, are governed by the culture and environment in which they find themselves.

For instance, after a giant engineering and electronics conglomerate paid $1.6 billion in 2008 to settle anti-bribery charges in the United States and Germany, the facts revealed that the company maintained an annual budget of between $40 million and $50 million for the express purpose of paying bribes to keep and win business. The headline in *The New York Times*—"Bribery Was Just a Line Item"—told the story. Investigators described bribery as the company's "business model," and when global anti-bribery laws became stricter, the organization created a "paper [anti-fraud] program" to cover its continuing illegal practices.

In this case, the company incentivized winning and maintaining business to the extent that it winked at law breaking, nurturing an environment in which corruption could flourish. In fact, the environment in which company employees worked led them to feel they were not acting abnormally but rather in the best interests of the business while protecting their colleagues' jobs.

A similar ecology existed at a large global retailer. To improve the appearance of profitability, its managers were pressured to conceal inventory shrinkage losses. The evolution of this practice has been blamed on the low staffing levels the company maintained, making accurate inventory management difficult. This established an environment of scarcity in which deceptive inventory processes were, at best, ignored by managers and, at worst, applauded, thereby discouraging those in charge from coming forward. In essence, the corporate ecology normalized financial statement fraud, creating fraudsters where, in a different environment, this might not have happened.

Deception need not be intentional nor a business strategy. In late 2012, a major European financial institution agreed to pay $1.9 billion in fines related to money laundering. According to the US Department of Justice, the bank laundered $881 million in drug profits and failed to invest in its anti-money laundering compliance programs. In 2009, it appointed an inexperienced director to run them. With substandard processes and governance, the bank basically was asleep at the switch, ignoring numerous red flags that otherwise would have alerted it to sketchy clients engaged in dubious transactions. By failing to understand and then to communicate the seriousness of the problem to its employees, the bank allowed these practices to continue and ultimately paid a steep price for snoozing.

An even steeper price was paid by another large European financial institution. In 2008 it admitted to a conspiracy to defraud the Internal Revenue Service (IRS), agreeing to pay $780 million in fines and to exit its highly profitable US wealth management business. As was the case with the engineering and electronics company, breaking the law seemed to have been part of the organization's business model. According to a whistleblower (who was ignored by the bank's chief compliance officer), the company had trained its employees to avoid detection in the US, equipped them with encrypted laptops, and incentivized them through bonuses and promotions to sell the company's products to United States clients without the proper licenses to do so.

The whistleblower, who ultimately was awarded $104 million by the IRS (the largest whistleblower award to date), described a culture that was insular, hierarchical and aggressively entrepreneurial, encouraging law breaking in the pursuit of profit even as its own policies declared the activities it promoted to be illegal. Not only would such a culture encourage fraudsters, it would attract them.

Creating a Fraud-Resistant Corporate Ecology

As noted, it's nearly impossible to predict whether any given individual will be inclined to commit fraud. However, the environment in which an employee works can be controlled by a company's leadership in both formal and informal ways to make fraud more difficult and cast it as an affront to the business's social norms. Most people wish to act as their colleagues do, and, therefore, if the corporate norm is one of zero tolerance for fraudulent activity, the commission of antisocial acts within the context of the business becomes, ideally, inconceivable. Companies must strive to make their offices and facilities places where it is hard for an individual to commit fraud and even harder to imagine that he or she could get away with it.

It is up to the company to establish a low-risk environment for fraud and provide incentives for ethical behavior by its executives, managers and employees. (According to the ACFE study, almost a fifth of reported frauds were perpetrated by owners/executives. Not surprisingly, ACFE found a high correlation between the organizational level of the fraudster and the financial impact of the fraud on the company; in other words, the higher up the fraudster, the more extensive the losses.)

Conduct a Risk Analysis

To begin creating a fraud-resistant environment and culture, companies must begin with a thorough risk analysis that should include a review of existing corporate policies, an analysis of internal compliance systems and processes, and an examination of the organization's communications strategies and practices. These reviews will enable leadership to assess the company's risk profile holistically. It should be kept in mind that various regions have different risk profiles, and organizations operating in multiple jurisdictions must conduct a risk assessment in each one.

This risk analysis should not be wholly quantitative since such a confined assessment would neither register nor reflect the ecology of the workplace. Ideally, an independent analyst, whose vision would not be clouded by the current culture, could provide open-minded leadership with an understanding of how people in the company are interacting, how managers are relating to employees and how informal information is shared in the workplace. Such an analysis could reveal where pockets of discontent exist, where dysfunctional behavior is tolerated and where there are cracks in more formal compliance processes—cracks that breed fraud. In effect, such an analyst would function as a corporate anthropologist, observing how people actually perform their job. This, as Harvard Business School's Tom Davenport has written, is the only way of "actually knowing what's happening and why in organizations."

A comprehensive risk analysis also must take into account the propensity for fraud in various departments. Accounting, for example, has the highest incidence of fraud, many times that of Legal and Research and Development, and, therefore, should be allotted commensurate attention. For instance, it makes sense to deploy tools and processes that monitor and double check billings, accounts receivable, collections and other accounting functions.

There are software systems that automatically provide warnings when, for example, a receipt or payment surfaces in excess of a given, predetermined amount and prevents an invoice from being processed without a designated manager's approval.

Although certain behavior—such as an employee living beyond his or her means or an HR report saying a worker is resistant to guidance or an executive demonstrating a wheeler-dealer mentality—can be an important red flag and part of building a risk profile, companies must be very careful not to fall victim to cultural biases or to be influenced by hidden agendas. Again, this points to the usefulness of engaging independent third parties to cross check these flagged individuals. Focusing on specific people, however, is of limited utility; what's critical is the overall ecology of the workplace in which these employees either succeed or fail.

Create a Transparency Forum

Much of the fraud in companies (as we've seen) is conducted by upper management. The only way to constrain undesirable conduct by executives is to increase the visibility of their actions.

Fraud is a shade-loving plant. Transparency creates an environment that's uncomfortable for fraudsters, making actions that hide illegal activity and information difficult. It would be wise for companies to invest in systems to ensure that transparency exists in the organization from top to bottom by making alerts, reviews and certain communications visible to employees at different levels of the company, whether via dedicated committees or individuals embedded in various functional areas. At the European financial institution, for example, the written policy that prohibited its wealth managers from selling its financial products on their business trips to the United States was hidden deep inside the corporate intranet. No one outside the compliance function knew of the policy's existence—certainly not the wealth managers—until it was discovered by accident by the whistleblower. Had that policy been broadly visible, the penalties levied on the bank might have been significantly less.

Be Alert to Cultural Red Flags

Employee dissatisfaction can point to deeper problems within an organization. At the aforementioned retailer, complaints about understaffing that overstretched employees—and made it hard for them to perform the accurate inventory counts that likely would have revealed the fraudulent reporting much earlier—should have been a warning signal to company leadership.

It, therefore, is critical for managers to enable qualitative, in-depth, anonymous interviews with employees on a regular basis. These interviews could be conducted by HR, but it generally is safer and more effective to look outside the company for a third party that can provide a less culturally proscribed picture. And lest these interviews be construed as invasive and needlessly time consuming, they should be conducted in as fluid and unintimidating manner as possible.

Inefficient communications—such as those that buried the European financial institution's cross-border business policy in its intranet—exposed the institution to large fines and loss of business. Dysfunctional management styles (unwarranted pressure on employees at the retailer) can encourage fraudulent activity, and the absence of compliance training even when policies are in place (such as they were at the engineering and electronics company) can lead companies astray. Corporate settings that lack clear policies or have policies that are poorly communicated and/or followed or that allow the immediate and long-term consequences of fraudulent activity to remain ambiguous or unstated are environments in which fraud is more likely to take root and flourish.

Have a Robust Whistleblower Program with Appropriate Protections

As the ACFE reported, almost half the tips that lead to fraud exposure come from employees. But merely having a whistleblower platform and encouraging people to come forward are only part of the equation. These whistleblowers also must be confident that the company will not turn on them. For example, at the retailer, some employees who brought their concerns about the inventory process to their managers allegedly were discharged later. And after the European financial institution whistleblower brought the Wealth Management division's policy violations to the attention of the bank's chief compliance officer, the whistleblower was denied a raise, was isolated and was advised by independent counsel to leave the company.

A robust whistleblower program is essential to creating an environment in which a fraudster will fear exposure, but without equally robust protection for a whistleblower, the program will be toothless.

The Sweet Spot: Where Ethics and Good Business Meet

Companies must vigorously instill an exemplary code of conduct at every level, not only because it's right to do so, but—in the current political environment in which governments and their regulatory agencies are becoming increasingly aggressive and less tolerant of violations—it's simply good business. Companies must not just talk the talk; they must walk the walk by implementing strong internal controls and establishing an ethical environment for conducting business. We have seen—with Enron and others—how quickly an unethical environment can destroy value for innocent stakeholders, as well as how swiftly a company can crumble.

The roots of a fraud rarely can be traced to a single unethical individual operating maliciously in a vacuum. A fraud is perpetrated when that person meets a specific environment. Companies can control those environments by defining both formal and informal rules and by understanding the mostly unseen, unexplored ecology of their organization. More than ever before, that understanding is not a "nice to have"; it's a "must have."

Reference
* "Report to the Nations on Occupational Fraud and Abuse," ACFE, 2014"

On Its Own, Whistleblowing Cannot Curb Corruption

Augusto Lopez-Claros

Previously an economics professor at the University of Chile, Dr. Augusto Lopez-Claros has worked with the World Bank Group and served as a senior fellow at the Edmund Walsh School of Foreign Service at Georgetown University.

Having looked at some of the ways in which corruption damages the social and institutional fabric of a country, we now turn to reform options open to governments to reduce corruption and mitigate its effects. Rose-Ackerman (1998) recommends a two-pronged strategy aimed at increasing the benefits of being honest and the costs of being corrupt, a sensible combination of reward and punishment as the driving force of reforms. This is a vast subject. We discuss below six complementary approaches.

Paying Civil Servants Well

Whether civil servants are appropriately compensated or grossly underpaid will clearly affect motivation and incentives. If public sector wages are too low, employees may find themselves under pressure to supplement their incomes in "unofficial" ways. Van Rijckeghem and Weder (2001) did some empirical work showing that in a sample of less developed countries, there is an inverse relationship between the level of public sector wages and the incidence of corruption.

Creating Transparency and Openness in Government Spending

Subsidies, tax exemptions, public procurement of goods and services, soft credits, extra-budgetary funds under the control

"Six Strategies to Fight Corruption," by Augusto Lopez-Claros, The World Bank Group, May 14, 2014. Reprinted by permission.

of politicians—all are elements of the various ways in which governments manage public resources. Governments collect taxes, tap the capital markets to raise money, receive foreign aid and develop mechanisms to allocate these resources to satisfy a multiplicity of needs. Some countries do this in ways that are relatively transparent and make efforts to ensure that resources will be used in the public interest. The more open and transparent the process, the less opportunity it will provide for malfeasance and abuse. Collier (2007) provides persuasive evidence on the negative impact of ineffective systems of budget control. Countries where citizens are able to scrutinize government activities and debate the merits of various public policies also makes a difference. In this respect, press freedoms and levels of literacy will, likewise, shape in important ways the context for reforms. Whether the country has an active civil society, with a culture of participation could be an important ingredient supporting various strategies aimed at reducing corruption.

New Zealand, which is consistently one of the top performers in Transparency International's *Corruption Perceptions Index*, is a pioneer in creating transparent budget processes, having approved in 1994 the Fiscal Responsibility Act, providing a legal framework for transparent management of public resources.

Cutting Red Tape

The high correlation between the incidence of corruption and the extent of bureaucratic red tape as captured, for instance, by the *Doing Business* indicators suggests the desirability of eliminating as many needless regulations while safeguarding the essential regulatory functions of the state. The sorts of regulations that are on the books of many countries—to open up a new business, to register property, to engage in international trade, and a plethora of other certifications and licenses—are sometimes not only extremely burdensome but governments have often not paused to examine whether the purpose for which they were introduced is at all relevant to the needs of the present. Rose-Ackerman (1998) suggests that "the most obvious approach is simply to eliminate laws and programs that breed corruption."

Replacing Regressive and Distorting Subsidies with Targeted Cash Transfers

Subsidies are another example of how government policy can distort incentives and create opportunities for corruption. According to an IMF study (2013), consumer subsidies for energy products amount to some $1.9 trillion per year, equivalent to about 2.5 percent of global GDP or 8 percent of government revenues. These subsidies are very regressively distributed, with over 60 percent of total benefits accruing to the richest 20 percent of households, in the case of gasoline. Removing them could result in a significant reduction in CO_2 emissions and generate other positive spillover effects. Subsidies often lead to smuggling, to shortages, and to the emergence of black markets. Putting aside the issue of the opportunity costs (how many schools could be built with the cost of one year's energy subsidy?), and the environmental implications associated with artificially low prices, subsidies can often put the government at the center of corruption-generating schemes. Much better to replace expensive, regressive subsidies with targeted cash transfers.

Establishing International Conventions

Because in a globalized economy corruption increasingly has a cross-border dimension, the international legal framework for corruption control is a key element among the options open to governments. This framework has improved significantly over the past decade. In addition to the OECD's Anti-Bribery Convention, in 2005 the UN Convention Against Corruption (UNCAC) entered into force, and by late 2013 had been ratified by the vast majority of its 140 signatories. The UNCAC is a promising instrument because it creates a global framework involving developed and developing nations and covers a broad range of subjects, including domestic and foreign corruption, extortion, preventive measures, anti-money laundering provisions, conflict of interest laws, means to recover illicit funds deposited by officials in offshore banks, among others. Since the UN has no enforcement powers, the effectiveness of the Convention as a tool to deter corruption will very much depend on the establishment of adequate national monitoring mechanisms to assess government compliance.

Others (Heinemann and Heimann (2006)) have argued that a more workable approach in the fight against corruption may consist of more robust implementation of the anticorruption laws in the 40 states that have signed the OECD's AntiBribery Convention. Governments will need to be more pro-active in cracking down on OECD companies that continue to bribe foreign officials. In their efforts to protect the commercial interests of national companies, governments have at times been tempted to shield companies from the need to comply with anticorruption laws, in a misguided attempt not to undermine their position vis-à-vis competitors in other countries. Trade promotion should not be seen to trump corruption control. Governments continue to be afflicted by double standards, criminalizing bribery at home but often looking the other way when bribery involves foreign officials in non-OECD countries.

Deploying Smart Technology

Just as government-induced distortions provide many opportunities for corruption, it is also the case that frequent, direct contact between government officials and citizens can open the way for illicit transactions. One way to address this problem is to use readily available technologies to encourage more of an arms-length relationship between officials and civil society; in this respect the Internet has been proved to be an effective tool to reduce corruption (Andersen *et al.*, 2011). In some countries the use of online platforms to facilitate the government's interactions with civil society and the business community has been particularly successful in the areas of tax collection, public procurement, and red tape. Perhaps one of the most fertile sources of corruption in the world is associated with the purchasing activities of the state. Purchases of goods and services by the state can be sizable, in most countries somewhere between 5-10 percent of GDP. Because the awarding of contracts can involve a measure of bureaucratic discretion, and because most countries have long histories of graft, kickbacks, and collusion in public procurement, more and more countries have opted for procedures that guarantee adequate levels of openness, competition, a level playing field for suppliers, fairly clear bidding procedures, and so on.

Chile is one country that has used the latest technologies to create one of the world's most transparent public procurement systems in the world. ChileCompra was launched in 2003, and is a public electronic system for purchasing and hiring, based on an Internet platform. It has earned a worldwide reputation for excellence, transparency and efficiency. It serves companies, public organizations as well as individual citizens, and is by far the largest business-to-business site in the country, involving 850 purchasing organizations. In 2012 users completed 2.1 million purchases issuing invoices totaling US$9.1 billion. It has also been a catalyst for the use of the Internet throughout the country.

In many of the measures discussed above aimed at combating corruption, the underlying philosophy is one of eliminating the opportunity for corruption by changing incentives, by closing off loopholes and eliminating misconceived rules that encourage corrupt behavior. But an approach that focuses solely on changing the rules and the incentives, accompanied by appropriately harsh punishment for violation of the rules, is likely to be far more effective if it is also supported by efforts to buttress the moral and ethical foundation of human behavior.

Organizations to Contact

The editor has compiled the following list of organizations concerned with the issues debated in this book. The descriptions are derived from materials provided by the organizations. All have publications or information available for interested readers. This list was compiled on the date of publication of the present volume; the information provided here may change. Be aware that many organizations take several weeks or longer to respond to inquiries, so allow as much time as possible.

Center for Constitutional Rights (CCR)
666 Broadway, 7th Floor
New York, NY 10012
phone: (212) 614-6464
website: www.ccrjustice.org

Rooted in civil and human rights, the CCR strives to uphold social justice using the law. Specifically, their "Corporate Human Rights Abuses" cause protects those who have been the victims of corporations in the US or beyond. Large corporations often have enough funding and backing from governments and other powerful entities, meaning that they are difficult to stop or sue if they violate human rights. The CCR pools resources to provide services for the most vulnerable across the international scene.

Centre for Free Expression (CFE)
Rogers Communications Centre
80 Gould Street
Toronto, Ontario M5B 2M7
Canada
phone: (416) 979-5000, ext. 6396
email: cfe@ryerson.ca
website: www.cfe.ryerson.ca

Based in Ontario, the CFE operates out of Ryerson University. Through partnering with other Canadian and international organizations, CFE facilitates advocacy and education centering around freedom of expression. Specifically, their movement for "Whistleblower Protection" fills the gaps left by Canadian legislation, which, they argue, can actually hinder rather than help whistleblowers. CFE focuses on raising awareness of exploitation and providing information to those interested in whistleblowing.

Instituto Mexicano de Derechos Humanos y Democracia (IMDHD)
Calle 9 90, San Pedro de los Pinos
03800 Ciudad de México
Mexico
website: www.imdhd.org

IMDHD is a human rights organization based in Mexico City. Founded in 2007, the organization utilizes a holistic approach to preserving human rights, considering the social, educational, political, and civil aspects of society. Their "Platforma Contral la Impunidad y la Corrupción" [Platform Against Impunity and Corruption] is an initiative that organizes various international organizations concerned with issues of corruption in Mexico.

National Whistleblower Center (NWC)
PO Box 25074
Washington, DC 20027
phone: (202) 342-1903
email: contact@whistleblowers.org
website: www.whistleblowers.org

The National Whistleblower Center is a nonprofit organization that serves as an advocate for individuals who plan to blow the whistle. A thirty-year-old agency, the NWC has long emphasized grassroots campaigns for the protections of whistleblowers. They partner with National Whistleblower Legal Defense and Education Fund (NWLDEF) to provide whistleblowers with lawyers. Finally, they have assisted in developing legislation that promotes the protection of whistleblowers, including the Dodd-Frank Act.

Office of the Public Sector Integrity Commissioner (PSIC)
60 Queen Street, 7th Floor
Ottawa ON, K1P 5Y7
Canada
phone: (613) 941-6400
website: www.psic.gc.ca

PSIC operates in the federal public sector, offering a channel by which to blow the whistle. The Commissioner will then initiate an investigation to determine the validity of the complaint. Aware that inappropriate whistleblowing occasionally takes place, the PSIC hopes to make sure that potential whistleblowers are well-informed by providing resources, definitions of terms, and language from various legislative strictures to readers on their website.

Project on Government Oversight (POGO)
1100 G Street NW, Suite 500
Washington DC, 20005-3806
phone: (202) 347-1122
email: info@pogo.org
website: www.pogo.org

The Project on Governmental Oversight is an organization that serves as a sort of institutional whistleblower. POGO operates as a watchdog, working to expose fraud, waste, and other misdeeds performed by the federal government. POGO aims to protect democracy by ensuring federal transparency and offering support for whistleblowers within the federal government.

US Merit Systems Protection Board (MSPB)
1615 M Street, NW
Washington, DC 20419
phone: (202) 254-4418
website: www.mspb.gov

MSPB is an independent agency that seeks to investigate fraud and other prohibited practices by encouraging federal employees to report issues through their organization. MSPB was established in 1978 as a part of the Civil Service Reform Act. It emphasizes that its duties are specific, and similar cases should be filed through other agencies, such as the Federal Labor Relations Authority (FLRA) and related organizations.

US Office of Special Council (OSC)
1730 M Street, NW, Suite 218
Washington, DC 20036-4505
phone: (202) 804-7000
website: www.osc.gov

The US Office of Special Council facilitates investigations and attempts to protect federal employees who experience reprisal after blowing the whistle. Serving as a mediator, the OSC deals with misconduct cases within the executive branch, which often fall under whistleblowing. The OSC offers several resources and services to those who hope to file a complaint or otherwise engage in whistleblowing.

WhistleblowersUK
Kemp House
152-160 City Road
London, EC1V 2NX
United Kingdom
phone: 07714 811547
website: www.wbuk.org

WhistleblowersUK is a nonprofit organization that not only assists whistleblowers in making their case, but also seeks to connect whistleblowers across the country. They have several hotlines for those involved in whistleblowing, as well as training for those going through the process. Like many other whistleblower-support organizations, they provide resources and advice for potential whistleblowers.

Bibliography

Books

C. Fred Alford. *Whistleblowers: Broken Lives and Organizational Power.* Ithaca, NY: Cornell University Press, 2001.

Carmen R. Apaza and Yongjin Chang, eds. *Whistleblowing in the World: Government Policy, Mass Media and the Law.* London, UK: Palgrave Macmillan, 2017.

Jennifer Arlen, ed. *Research Handbook on Corporate Crime and Financial Misdealing.* Northampton, MA: Edward Elgar Publishing, 2018.

Angie Ash. *Whistleblowing and Ethics in Health and Social Care.* London, UK: Jessica Kingsley Publishers, 2016.

David Callahan. *The Cheating Culture: Why More Americans Are Doing Wrong to Get Ahead.* New York, NY: Houghton Mifflin, 2004.

Emanuela Ceva and Michele Bocchiola. *Is Whistleblowing a Duty?* Medford, MA: Polity Press, 2019.

Cynthia Cooper. *Extraordinary Circumstances: The Journey of a Corporate Whistleblower.* Hoboken, NJ: John Wiley & Sons, 2008.

Falko C. Daub. *New Whistleblowing Regulations in the U.S.A.: How Sarbanes-Oxley failed to implement a working concept.* Saarbruken, Germany: VDM Verlag Dr. Mueller, 2007.

Dennis Gentilin. *The Origins of Ethical Failures.* London: Routledge, 2016.

Mark Hertsgaard. *Bravehearts: Whistle-Blowing in the Age of Snowden.* New York, NY: Skyhorse Publishing, 2016.

Roberta Ann Johnson. *Whistleblowing: When it Works—and Why.* Boulder, CO: Lynne Reinner Publishers, 2003.

Kate Kenny. *Whistleblowing: Toward a New Theory.* Cambridge, MA: Harvard University Press, 2019.

Stephen Martin Kohn. *The New Whistleblower's Handbook: A Step-By-Step Guide to Doing What's Right and Protecting Yourself.* Lanham, MD: Rowman and Littlefield, 2017.

Frederick D. Lipman. *Whistleblowers: Incentives, Disincentives, and Protection Strategies.* Hoboken, NJ: John Wiley and Sons, 2012.

Sarah Myhill. *Sustainable Medicine: Whistle-Blowing on 21st-Century Medical Practice.* London, UK: Hammersmith Books, 2015.

Paul Van Buitenen. *Blowing the Whistle: One Man's Fight Against Fraud in the European Commission.* London, UK: Politico's Publishing Ltd., 2000.

Periodicals and Internet Sources

Vishal P. Baloria, Carol Marquardt, and Christine I. Wiedman, "A Lobbying Approach to Evaluating the Whistleblower Provisions of the Dodd-Frank Reform Act of 2010," *SSRN Electronic Journal*, May 2013. https://papers.ssrn.com/sol3/papers.cfm?abstract_id=1923310.

Andrew C. Call, Gerald S. Martin, Nathan Y. Sharp, and Jarod H. Wilde, "Whistleblowers and Outcomes of Financial Misrepresentation Enforcement Actions," *Journal of Accounting Research*, May 5, 2017. https://doi.org/10.1111/1475-679X.12177.

Naomi Colvin, "Whistle-Blowing As a Form of Digital Resistance: State Crimes and Crimes Against the State," *State Crime*, Vol. 7, Number 1 (24-45), Spring 2018. https://www.researchgate.net/publication/327872675_Whistle-Blowing_as_a_Form_of_Digital_Resistance_State_Crimes_and_Crimes_Against_the_State.

James Charles Crowley, "Want to Be a Whistleblower? Read This First," *Chicago Tribune*, April 23, 2018. www. chicagotribune.com. https://www.chicagotribune.com/ news/opinion/commentary/ct-perspec-whistleblower-wall-street-supreme-court-0423-20180420-story.html.

David F. Engstrom, "Public Regulation of Private Enforcement: Empirical Analysis of DOJ Oversight of Qui Tam Litigation Under the False Claims Act," *Northwestern University Law Review*, 107, 1689–1756.

Laura McLellan, "Should Employers Offer Financial Incentives for Whistleblowing," *Employment Law Worldview*, January 19, 2015. https://www.employmentlawworldview. com/should-employers-offer-financial-incentives-for-whistleblowing/.

Jensen T. Mecca, Vincent Giorgini, Kelsey Medeiros, Carter Gibson, Lynn Devenport, Shane Connelly, and Michael Mumford, "Perspectives on Whistleblowing: Faculty Member Viewpoints and Suggestions for Organizational Change," *Accountability in Research: Policies and Quality Assurance*, Vol. 21, Issue 3 (159-175), December 10, 2013. https://doi.org/10.1080/08989621.2014.847735.

Theo Nyreröd and Giancarlo Spagnolo, "Myths and Numbers on Whistleblower Rewards," *Stockholm Institute of Transition Economics*, Working Paper No. 44, December 1, 2017. https://papers.ssrn.com/sol3/papers.cfm?abstract_id=3100754.

Frederik Obermaier and Bastian Obermayer, "Whistleblowers Are Vital to Democracy. We Need to Better Protect Them," *Los Angeles Times*, April 9, 2018. https://www.latimes.com/ opinion/op-ed/la-oe-obermaier-obermayer-whistleblowers-20180409-story.html.

David Schultza and Khachik Harutyunyan, "Combating Corruption: The Development of Whistleblowing Laws in the United States, Europe, and Armenia," *Elsevier B.V.*, Vol. 2, Issue 2, (87-97), December 2015.

Anne Kates Smith, "The Elusive Rewards and High Costs of Being a Whistleblower," *Kiplinger Washington*, June 2013. https://www.kiplinger.com/article/business/T012-C000-S002-high-costs-of-being-a-whistleblower.html.

Steven Davidoff Solomon, "Whistle-Blower Awards Lure Wrongdoers Looking to Score," *New York Times*, December 30, 2014. https://dealbook.nytimes.com/2014/12/30/whistle-blower-awards-lure-wrongdoers-looking-to-score/.

Jaron H. Wilde, "The Deterrent Effect of Employee Whistleblowing on Firms' Financial Misreporting and Tax Aggressiveness," the *Accounting Review*: Vol. 92, Number 5 (247-280), September 2017. https://doi.org/10.2308/accr-51661.

Index

A

Abu Ghraib, 38
Addison, Wendy, 102–103, 108–110
anonymous reporting, 27–29, 32, 53–56, 104–106, 111
  accountability, 54–55
  benefits, 53–54
  feedback checklist, 55–56
Anti-Bribery Convention, 27, 185
Association of Certified Fraud Examiners (ACFE), 23, 173–175, 178–179, 181
Australian Signals Directorate, 96
Australian Treasure Laws Amendment (Whistleblowers) Bill, 110
Autorite des marches financiers (AMF), 31

B

Bastion, Laura, 63
Bittler, Thomas, 78
Booz Allen Hamilton, 92
Boundless Informant, 93
British Public Interest Disclosure Act, 152
Brown & Williamson, 22–23

C

Central Alabama Veterans Health Care System, 156–160
CIA, 40, 92
Civil War (US), 22, 106, 113, 145
Cooper, Cynthia, 58, 59, 61, 65–66, 67
corporate compliance programs, 134–141
corruption, 15–16, 24–33, 84–89, 134–141, 142–147, 148–155, 164–172, 183–187

D

data breach, 46–47, 51
Dodd-Frank Wall Street Reform and Consumer Protection Act (Dodd-Frank Act), 19, 30, 36, 85–86, 106, 112, 134–137, 138–141

E

Embraer SA, 26
Enron, 57, 59, 62, 65, 113, 182
ethical considerations, 18–20, 182